Supernatural EYESIGHT

Seeing Through The Eyes Of The Holy Spirit

Morris Cerullo

TABLE OF CONTENTS

FOREWARD

"And when the servant of the man of God was risen early, and gone forth, behold, an host compassed the city both with horses and chariots. And his servant said unto him, Alas, my master! how shall we do? And he answered, Fear not: for they that be with us are more than they that be with them. And Elisha prayed, and said, LORD, I pray thee, open his eyes, that he may see. And the LORD opened the eyes of the young man; and he saw: and, behold, the mountain was full of horses and chariots of fire round about Elisha."

2 Kings 6:15-17

When we read this story, we see the familiar story of the man who can't see God and can't understand the things in the spirit.

Now, we notice that the prophet said, "Lord, open his eyes."

The implication is clear: the servant's eyes were CLOSED.

But what eyes are the scripture talking about?

The prophet asked God to open the servant's eyes "that he may see."

But it's clear from the servant's words that he has eyesight: he can see that the enemy's forces are gathered around them.

So the prophet is not asking God to give sight to a blind servant.

What eyes are the prophet wanting opened?

The rest of the story tells us what eyes the prophet is talking about.

When the servant's eyes are opened, he sees the things that were happening in the spirit all around him but he was completely oblivious to.

The reality of life is that the spiritual world is alive, vibrant and ever active around us as we go about our day-to-day lives.

We just don't see it because, like the prophet's servant, our eyes have not been opened.

When his eyes were opened, the servant saw what the prophet saw all along — the hosts of God were around them, active and prepared to defend them.

Supernatural eyesight is looking into the spirit, as the prophet Elisha did, and seeing the spiritual reality that is hidden from natural eyes.

That supernatural eyesight is essential to the higher calling of the Christian. It is absolutely necessary that we understand it and learn how to ignore what the physical eyes are telling us so that we can see what God is revealing to us through the supernatural eyes.

As you read this book, you will find many revelation truths that you may not have considered before. Those truths are the key to understanding things God's way — in the Spirit.

As you go through this book's pages, let God reveal to you the supernatural truths He has prepared for you.

It is not by accident that you have picked this book up — it is a divine appointment with destiny.

When you finish the final page, you and I will have been through a journey together — a journey into the Spirit.

Are you ready? Let's go.

Morris Cerullo

CHAPTER ONE

EYES THAT SEE;
EARS THAT HEAR

As the gazelle grazes on the grasses of the African plains, it keeps a watchful eye out for predators.

The gazelle is not much bigger than your average-sized dog, and it's apparently pretty tasty, so it is on constant vigil against the ever-present threat of its enemy.

To assist it, God gave the gazelle incredible advantages — it is lightning-quick, and can dart off at the slightest indication of danger.

But even more amazing than speed that can sometimes dazzle even the world's fastest land predator — the cheetah — the gazelle's most important defensive advantage is its eyes. With one eye on either side of its head, the little animal can see nearly 360 degrees at one time — in other words, it's impossible to sneak up from behind it.

Its ears also whirl around like a periscope, catching sounds from literally any direction, always listening for the crack of the underbrush, the distress cry of another gazelle, or the quickened panting of a hungry lioness creeping through the tall grass.

Despite these tremendous advantages, however, if the gazelle does not have a significant head start on a predator, chances are slim that it will escape becoming lunch for a hungry pride of lions or a pack of hyenas.

The predators have their own advantages. Almost all predators have what scientists call stereoscopic vision — their eyes are forward-set, and one is slightly higher than the other, allowing the predator to accurately judge speed and distance between itself and its prey.

Though the predator cannot see behind itself as the gazelle can, it most often doesn't need to — it's the one doing the hunting.

As the predator closes in on its target, the stereoscopic vision allows it to hone in and grab at the target, deftly avoiding sharp horns and hoofs that are the prey's last resort of desperation.

Each animal's eyes and ears are perfectly designed to serve its purposes — the prey's eyes and ears are designed for defense and early warning. The predator's are designed to aid in hunting, grabbing and killing.

As humans — in the natural — God designed us as predators. Our eyes are forward-set, allowing us to zoom in on our prey.

But God's designs for humans go beyond the physical. He created us unlike the animals. We are able to worship, to pray and to have a relationship with the living God. We are fundamentally different than the animals — we are spiritual beings created that way in God's image (after all, He is Spirit).

He has equipped our natural bodies with the eyes and ears most suited to our needs as omnivores (meaning we eat both plants and animals).

But He has equipped our spiritual selves even more appropriately — the needs of our spiritual man differ from our natural man.

The natural man needs to eat physical food or it will die.

The spiritual man needs to feed from the Word or it will die.

To get the physical food, the natural man must have eyes and ears designed to enable him to hunt.

To get the spiritual food, the spiritual man must have eyes to see and ears to hear what the Spirit is saying!

All truth is parallel. What is true in the natural has a parallel truth in the spirit — we can learn a lot about God and His nature by learning about the natural world He created.

Many Christians silently suffer with guilt and self-condemnation for one reason: they don't hear from God as clearly as they think they should.

Christians hear so many people, ministers and laymen alike, who talk about hearing from God, speaking to God and receiving directions from God. And many times, when Christians don't hear from God like they hear other people are, they begin to feel guilty, as if God has judged their walk with Him and found it lacking — and therefore is keeping silent.

I want to tell you right now, before we get into the deep, incredible revelations God has given in the rest of this book, that comparing yourself to other Christians is begging for trouble:

"But they measuring themselves by themselves, and comparing themselves among themselves, are not wise."
2 Corinthians 10:12

Deep revelation into God's Word and His nature is not reserved for the very few. God has not chosen three or four people to understand the deep things of Him, excluding all others.

His understanding is open to all who will come to Him.

Indeed, the Bible says it this way:

"For there is no respect of persons with God."

Romans 2:11

That's God saying He doesn't look to just a few people and give them the good things — He's prepared to give it to all who will come to Him.

God revealed that to me in a profound way in 1962, when He asked me what I wanted out of ministry and life.

The answer welled up from deep in my soul — that's how I know it came from God, and not from me.

My answer to God was this: "God, give me the ability to take what you've given me, and give it to someone else."

I understood by the Spirit of God that He had not called me to be on a high horse somewhere, speaking down to people who could not understand without me telling them God's will.

Instead, He had called me to be an instrument in His hand, bringing people along where God had led me — He wanted me to impart the same anointing that is on my life into theirs.

That's why Paul can so boldly state: *"Be ye followers of me, even as I also am of Christ."*   *1 Corinthians 11:1*

Paul wanted the believers to be where he was — he wanted them to understand what he understood.

When Jesus was working tremendous miracles, He told the disciples something incredible:

"He that believeth on me, the works that I do shall he do also; and greater works than these shall he do."
John 14:12

God has designed you — as a born-again believer — to work GREATER works than Jesus worked.

Friend, there's a fundamental understanding that will change your life if you believe you'll work greater works than Jesus worked:

"The Son can do nothing of himself, but what he seeth the Father do: for what things soever he doeth, these also doeth the Son likewise."
John 5:19

Here's the understanding (you may want to take out a highlighter marker and mark this statement): Jesus said He worked His works by seeing in the Spirit the Father working those works first. THEN HE PROMISED YOU'D DO GREATER WORKS!

To do greater works, you must SEE GREATER WORKS IN THE SPIRIT! You must see into the supernatural and, with the supernatural eyesight God has given you, you will see greater works and work them in the natural!

Jesus never did anything except He first saw in the Spirit His Father doing them first.

For Him, supernatural eyesight was the foundational principle upon which His actions were based. He did not just wander about, working miracles because He had the power to do so. Instead, He observed, and then He acted.

The reason many Christians don't find themselves working the works of God is because they have not first developed their supernatural eyesight, seeing the things in the Spirit that they should do in the natural.

Many people look in the Bible, and they believe the words printed on the page are the depth of its power.

But the depth of the power of the Word is the fact that it is ALIVE! Without supernatural eyesight, the words are just words on a page. In fact, Jesus said as much:

*"Ye **have not his word** abiding in you: for whom he hath sent, him ye believe not. Search the scriptures; **for in them ye think ye have eternal** life: and they are they which testify of me."*   *John 5:38-39*

The religious leaders to whom Jesus was speaking made a lifestyle out of knowing the words of God's revelation to mankind.

They studied the Scriptures on a daily basis, singing the words to help them better remember them. They treated the word with great reverence, even regulating that a boy could not touch the scrolls that contained the words until he had reached a certain age and passed certain tests.

They took great care to copy the words from scroll to scroll so that even one letter would not be lost in the transcribing. They counted the words, counted the letters, made sure everything was just perfect, or they destroyed the copy upon which they had been working for months.

They wrote the words on tiny pieces of paper and wore them on their heads and their hands.

They debated and revered the word to the point that none would ever dare challenge a master of the words.

But with all that study, with all that reading, with all that knowledge of the words that were on the page, Jesus rebuked those diligent and zealous students of the words He Himself had inspired.

They knew the words, but they didn't have the Word abiding in their hearts.

Without the Spirit — without the supernatural eyesight — knowing the words was as useless to them as knowing the words to a children's lullaby.

The words themselves communicated a message — and it was the message, not the words, that was important. That message was a message of Spirit.

Without seeing into the Spirit, they would forever be in the dark, paying attention to the words without ever catching their message — or as the old idiom goes, they were missing the forest because they were looking at all the trees.

Paul put it this way:
"For what the law could not do, in that it was weak through the flesh, God sending his own Son in the likeness of sinful flesh, and for sin, condemned sin in the flesh: That the righteousness of the law might be fulfilled in us, who walk not after the flesh, but after the Spirit. For they that are after the flesh do mind the things of the flesh; but they that are after the Spirit the things of the Spirit. For to be carnally minded is death; but to be spiritually minded

*is life and peace. Because the carnal mind is enmity
against God: for it is not subject to the law of God, neither
indeed can be. So then they that are in the flesh cannot
please God."*   Romans 8:3-8

To truly understand the spiritual things, we must have
supernatural eyesight — we must see the things in the
Spirit that our spiritual eyes were designed to see.

Understand me: when I say "see in the Spirit" what I
mean is "understand what the Spirit is saying."

So without understanding what the Spirit is saying, the
words of the Scripture are just words — the power comes
when the Spirit brings those words to LIFE.

Isaiah saw a striking difference between the God he had
read about and the living God one day:

*"In the year that king Uzziah died I saw also the
LORD sitting upon a throne, high and lifted up, and his
train filled the temple. Above it stood the seraphims:
each one had six wings; with twain he covered his face,
and with twain he covered his feet, and with twain he
did fly. And one cried unto another, and said, Holy,
holy, holy, is the LORD of hosts: the whole earth is full
of his glory. And the posts of the door moved at the
voice of him that cried, and the house was filled with
smoke. Then said I, Woe is me! for I am undone;
because I am a man of unclean lips, and I dwell in the
midst of a people of unclean lips: for mine eyes have
seen the King, the LORD of hosts. Then flew one of the
seraphims unto me, having a live coal in his hand,
which he had taken with the tongs from off the altar:
And he laid it upon my mouth, and said, Lo, this hath
touched thy lips; and thine iniquity is taken away, and
thy sin purged. Also I heard the voice of the Lord,*

*saying, Whom shall I send, and who will go for us? Then
said I, Here am I; send me."*   *Isaiah 6:1-8*

When the man of God saw the God he served, his
perception was radically altered.

As the mighty angels shook the very foundations of the
building with the force of their praises to the living God,
the prophet gained a stark realization that the holiness of
the God he was serving is absolute. He understood a new
depth of the power and greatness of God. He understood
by the very vehemence of the praises of the angels that
God was nobody to be trifled with.

And immediately he understood: woe is me! I have
unclean lips and my people have unclean lips — and yet
I'm in the presence of the holy God of Israel!

This vision of supernatural eyesight forever radically
changed the life of Isaiah.

He saw a glimpse of the Father in His glory.

Remember, what Isaiah saw had to be only a glimpse,
because the full depth of God's glory would kill any
mortal man. Exodus 33:20

Only Jesus has seen the full glory of the Father — but
what Isaiah saw was enough to change him forever.

He had a glimpse into the supernatural.

But God was not done at the call of Isaiah. He went on,
and demonstrated that He knew all along how men would
blind their own eyes to His truth.

*"And he said, Go, and tell this people, Hear ye
indeed, but understand not; and see ye indeed, but*

perceive not. Make the heart of this people fat, and make their ears heavy, and shut their eyes; lest they see with their eyes, and hear with their ears, and understand with their heart, and convert, and be healed."

Isaiah 6:9-10

This is a clear description of the nature of man.

Because a man has eyes, he says that he can see.

Because he has ears, he says he can hear.

Because he has the Word, he says he knows God and His will.

But God says the men will see, but they will not understand. They will hear, but they will not be able to understand what they're hearing.

The fact is, the greatest hindrance often to hearing and seeing the supernatural is that men don't want to see and hear the supernatural.

They say they want to, but in their hearts, they know that seeing in the supernatural by necessity brings about a change in their lives. They must repent, and as the passage in Isaiah said, "be converted."

Because of this hardness of their hearts, God told the prophet Isaiah to go and preach so that, by ignoring God's Word, their seeing eyes would be made blind, their hearing ears deaf and their heart be made fat.

This is the sad state in which many people find themselves.

But when we read such an indictment, we tend to immediately begin thinking of sinners — of the "unchurched," so to speak.

We wag our heads and grumble about how the sinners will never open their hearts to receive the Gospel, will never listen though the clear signs are right in front of their eyes.

The church loves to look at the world and hiss through its teeth at the heathen who refuse to hear the Word of God and see the truth.

And all the while the church is patting itself on the back for its ability to "see the truth," the cold, hard fact is that the people with eyes that don't see and ears that don't hear are more often than not those who call themselves Christians.

When Christians take time to see that the vast majority of preaching in the New Testament was aimed not at sinners, but at religious leaders, they're shocked.

When they see Jesus calling people "hypocrites," it's not the sinners He's talking to — its "church folks" — people who claim to be following Him, but just as the religious leaders of His day, they know the words, but don't have Him living in their hearts.

Their eyes are firmly focused on the natural things — the world around them, the physical world, their physical needs, their physical desires.

They can no more see in the Spirit than the man on the moon — and yet they're claiming to be leaders.

That was why Jesus' admonition to Nicodemus seemed so harsh:

"Marvel not that I said unto thee, Ye must be born again. The wind bloweth where it listeth, and thou

*hearest the sound thereof, but canst not tell whence it cometh, and whither it goeth: so is every one that is born of the Spirit. Nicodemus answered and said unto him, How can these things be? Jesus answered and said unto him, **Art thou a master of Israel, and knowest not these things?**"*   *John 3:7-10*

Jesus made a clear dividing line here — those who are born of flesh, who are natural men, follow the rules and norms of the natural. Everyone knows where they're coming from and where they're going.

Those who are born of the Spirit, however, are supernatural — they follow a living Spirit, and nobody knows where they're coming from or where they're going.

Then Jesus admonished Nicodemus: how is it that you call yourself a teacher, a rabbi, and you don't understand these things?

The same call goes out to the Church today: how can Christians pretend to know the truth when they don't understand the fundamental truth of the Spirit?

Remember, Jesus said that, as Christians, we are no longer of this world — we are aliens. We're not called anymore to follow the directions of the world, to keep its rules of nature, to follow its laws of physics. We are from another world and we're headed back there!

If we can see past the natural world and the natural understanding, we will have a keen insight into the Spirit — supernatural eyesight!

Just as our bodies are designed to seek the answers to their own needs through their natural eyesight, our spirits are designed to seek the answers to their needs in the Spirit.

That supernatural eyesight is not something you can drum up.

It's not something you can say a few words and expect to happen.

It's not something you can pretend to have and expect it to just plop down in your lap because of your diligence.

Supernatural eyesight is a FUNDAMENTAL BYPRODUCT of the born-again, Spirit-led life.

But just as in the natural, it must be trained, honed and perfected through practice.

When a natural baby is born, it has trouble focusing its eyes very tightly. But as it uses its eyes more, they become stronger, more adept, more able to focus and hone in.

When the spiritual baby is born, it can see, but it must practice to develop the eyesight in the supernatural.

It must learn to discern the things the Spirit is saying.

The admonitions of the Book of Revelation from Jesus were not to sinners. They were to the Church.

They were to Christians.

So when the Bible speaks of those whose "candlesticks" might be removed, it's not speaking to those who have never accepted Jesus. It's speaking to those who have accepted Him but are not working His works.

And remember, earlier in this chapter, you marked a paragraph that said Jesus only worked those works He first saw His father do. Then He said you would work greater

works, implying that you would see into the Spirit realm
and work the works you see your Father do.

Here's what Jesus said to the churches in Asia:

*"He that hath an ear, let him hear what the Spirit saith
unto the churches..."*   *Revelation 2:7*

He doesn't say "let everyone hear what the Spirit saith..."

He says that those WHO ARE LISTENING will hear.

This is the fundamental truth that is so difficult for
many to understand.

Many listen, but they don't hear what they want to hear,
so they ignore what the Spirit is saying.

But, much as the gazelle I talked about earlier in this
chapter, if a Christian only pays attention to the sounds he
likes to hear or the sights he likes to see, he will find
himself being a quick snack for his enemy.

The gazelle may not want to hear the warning sounds that
come to his ears as the grass crackles under his enemy's
feet. He may not want to see the telltale signs of an
indention in the overgrown weeds moving slowly his way.

But those things are signs that God has provided to give
the gazelle a head start — to let him use the natural
defenses God has given him to overcome his enemy.

Similarly, in the spirit, many Christians do not want to
hear what God has to say. When they hear the gentle
wooing of the Holy Spirit, they may not want to be stirred
up. When they see the profound revelations of God's
word, they may not want to be moved out of their comfort
zone and into the realm of the living Word.

But those things are works God has provided for the supernatural endowment of our spirit man to fulfill the purpose for which God created us in His image.

When God says He's looking for people who have ears to hear and eyes to see, He's looking for people who will heed Him even when what He says may not have been what they wanted to hear.

When God spoke to Isaiah, His words were frightening. They were words of doom and gloom for the nation of Israel.

But God knew that, as much as Isaiah didn't want to hear the words, he would act on them, he would do what God wanted him to do, and he would be moved in the spirit.

I believe that by very virtue of getting this far along in this book, you also want to hear from God — you want to develop your supernatural eyesight and act on God's word, even if it's not what you wanted to hear.

Keep this in mind: Jesus, as I mentioned earlier, only did the things He saw His Father doing first.

And when He allowed those who hated Him to seize Him, mock Him, pluck the beard from His face, abuse Him, crucify Him and stab Him with a spear, it was because His Father first had endured mocking, abuse and hatred from mankind for thousands of years.

And so, though He had power to calm the wind and the waves, heal the sick, bring sight to the blind, cast out devils, raise the dead, walk on water, feed thousands and confound the best of His critics, Jesus — as His Father had — allowed Himself to be abused at the hands of those He had created.

Supernatural eyesight is that — it's having the power to literally change the world around you, but engaging in that power not for the sake of the power itself, but because your Father first showed you to do it.

Do Christians have the power to move mountains? ABSOLUTELY YES!

Do Christians have the ability to control the weather? ABSOLUTELY YES!

Do Christians have the power to force the very laws of nature and physics to obey their commands? WITHOUT A DOUBT.

But that power comes as a result of seeing into the spirit realm and seeing what our Father is doing — and doing as we see Him do.

This is the foundation and basis for supernatural eyesight.

If you have ever looked at a man or woman of God and wondered how they achieved their tremendous insight into God's Word and His nature, the answer is in the rest of this book.

If you have looked at the saints of old in the Bible — both in the Old and New Testaments — and wondered where they came up with their faith, their understanding of the nature of God, the rest of this book will reveal their secrets to you.

As you learn these mysteries of the Gospel, understand that this is not a "how to" book; supernatural eyesight is a result of the indwelling Holy Spirit working His power in your life, teaching you, guiding you and leading you in the ways of God from time immemorial.

It's as Jesus promised: "But the Comforter, which is the Holy Ghost, whom the Father will send in my name, he shall teach you all things, and bring all things to your remembrance, whatsoever I have said unto you."

John 14:26

No "how to" book can replace the living, indwelling action of the Holy Spirit. It is His place to bring about incredible understanding of the deep things of God in your life.

This book is designed to deepen your understanding of the underlying foundations of supernatural eyesight.

Just as the lion uses her natural eyes to hone in on her target, this book will teach you to, as the Bible says, have a single eye toward your goal — supernatural eyesight.

CHAPTER TWO

THE UNBELIEVABLE WISDOM OF JOB

If we talk about supernatural eyesight, we cannot overlook the amazing insight of the wisdom of Job.

We know very little about Job's life other than what is recorded in the book that bears his name.

We don't know where he learned about God. We don't know how he got his tremendous understanding.

But what we do know is that Job has a tremendous understanding of God.

Job is widely believed to be a contemporary of the patriarch Abraham, meaning he lived at or near the time of Abraham.

His book is believed to be the oldest book of the Bible, written hundreds of years before Genesis was written.

What we do know is that Job had a tremendous grasp of both the nature and the Gospel of God.

Many times, we use the book of Job to teach about the nature of the devil's place on earth. In the first two chapters, we learn that the devil accuses Job, a righteous man, before God, and God allows the devil to tempt Job.

But the lessons of the book of Job are much deeper than that.

Other times, we use the book to learn about perseverance; if we persevere through temptation, we will be blessed many times over for what we lost.

These lessons are the two most prominent lessons we take from the book of Job.

But the lessons of this book are much deeper. There are two major lessons to be learned from Job.

The second major lesson we take from Job is that man is not more righteous than God; man's wisdom is out of its depth in challenging God's wisdom. Man is wrong in second-guessing the motives of God.

Notice that I did not say man is wrong in questioning God.

In fact, God says in Isaiah chapter 1: "Come now, and let us reason together..."

God is not afraid to be questioned on His nature, His actions, His ways or almost anything else. But challenging His motives is folly — it is the height of pride of man.

Job, however, teaches us that his understanding of God is both profound and far-reaching.

Most of us are familiar with the basic story behind Job. He was a righteous and perfect man, according to the beginning of the book. Satan came to God and asked God to allow him to tempt Job. In the course of tempting him, Satan killed Job's children, took away his riches and devastated Job's health.

As Job is mourning, his wife tells him to cast aside his integrity, curse God and die.

Of course, Job — being a righteous man — refuses.

But the bulk of the book comes when three of Job's friends come for the dubious reason of trying to comfort him.

It's really a misnomer to call the three Job's friends, given their embarrassing treatment of him.

In fact, the Hebrew word translated "friend" in describing the three actually means "associate."

The three associates are Eliphaz, Bildad and Zophar. It sounds like a law firm, but with the way they represent Job, they would never win a case in court.

Eliphaz's name means "God of gold."

Bildad's name means "Bel has loved." In case you're wondering, "Bel" was the god of the Babylonians.

Zophar's name means "departing."

Eliphaz is the first of the friends to "console" Job. He starts out by telling Job that the innocent don't suffer.

"Those who plow iniquity and sow misery reap the same." (Job 4:8 direct translation from the Hebrew Masoretic Text)

What he's really saying is: "Job, you're in this situation because you have been unrighteous. You are reaping what you sowed. You sowed sinfulness, and now you're reaping sinfulness."

He continues by saying God doesn't put any trust in His servants, and God can't really hear us anyway. Here's what he says:

"Call now. Is there anyone answering you?"   Job 5:1

Eliphaz does not believe God will answer Job. He does not believe in a God who's interested and involved in the lives of His people. Trouble doesn't happen all by itself, Eliphaz says. There has to be a cause — to him, Job must have done something to bring this evil upon himself. Repent, he tells Job, and you'll prosper. Everything will go well for you; you'll have God's favor. Indeed, "You shall know that your seed will be numerous, and your offspring as the grass of the earth. You shall come to the grave in full vigor, like a stack of grain comes up in its season. Consider this. We have searched it out; it is so. Hear it, and know it for yourself."   Job 5:24-27

To add insult to injury, he seeks to add legitimacy to his attempt to blame Job for his own troubles by saying "we've figured this all out. Learn from me!"

How many of us would love to have a friend like that?

But how many times have we heard the gospel of Eliphaz? "Oh, so and so is having such a tough time. I wonder what he did wrong."

Job answers Eliphaz like this: "Show me where I've done wrong, and I'll agree with you. You're an empty bag of wind. Some friend you are! You're digging a pit for your friend."

Job's saying, hey, you're talking in generalities. You know me — you're my associate. Where did I sin that this befell me? Show me.

Bildad adds insult to injury by reinforcing the message of Eliphaz: *"If you were pure and upright, surely now He (God) would rise for you and make whole the abode of your righteousness."*   Job 8:6

Now, this is a fancy way of saying, "you're full of it, Job. If you were righteous as you claim, God would jump into action and fix everything that's wrong. The fact that He's leaving you in trouble is proof positive that you're full of sin! Stop trying to paint yourself as Mr. Righteous and repent!"

Job answers the accusation by preaching the Gospel thousands of years before the New Testament was written: *"...how can a man be just with God? If he would argue with Him, he cannot answer Him one of a thousand." (9:2-3) "Though I were righteous, I could not answer Him; I seek mercy for my judgment." (9:15)*

Job has a profound understanding of the nature of salvation! Even if I am righteous, I can't stand before God and answer His questions! I can't stand before Him! I can't look righteous in His sight — I have to depend on MERCY! He further says: *"If I justify myself, my mouth will condemn me; though I am perfect, He shall declare me perverse." (9:20)*
He's saying, you guys don't understand! The actions of my body cannot win approval from God! If I stand before Him and claim righteousness through my actions, He will call my bluff and pronounce me a sinner! I depend on mercy to justify me!

This is the most succinct picture of the Gospel recorded in the Old Testament! Even if we behave PERFECTLY, we are perverse! As Isaiah later says, my righteousness is as filthy rags in His sight!

It is mercy that justifies us!

Partner, Job's understanding of the nature of God is both profound and astounding. Where did he learn these things? The Bible does not tell us.

Zophar, however, is much as the Pharisees in the New Testament. His idea of righteousness is the same as theirs — righteousness through works and rewards in this life. In chapter 11, he says that if Job will do away with his iniquity, everything will be all right! Notice, Zophar, just as the others, stresses that Job can make everything right. In verse 6, he says, *"Know then that God forgets some of your iniquity for you."* But, lest we think he's about to agree with Job, in verse 14, he says:

"if iniquity is in your hand, put it far away and do not let wickedness dwell in your tents; surely then you shall lift up your face without blemish; and you will be steadfast, and will not fear. For you shall forget your misery and shall remember it as waters that have passed."
Job 11:14-16

Now, I don't have any intentions of offending anyone just for the purpose of offending them, but I think someone might be offended by this statement: Zophar's statement is the gospel that's preached by many claiming to represent Christ! They tell you that God will forgive what you've done already — just come to the cross and say this prayer with me. But now that you've been forgiven, you've got to put iniquity far away from you.

The emphasis is that YOU'VE got to make a move. The impetus is on you. God did His part, now you've got to do yours. The Bible tells us that Jesus Himself will form righteousness in us through the indwelling, but the gospel of Zophar is that you earn righteousness through your actions.

This is the gospel of Zophar, straight from the mouth of the false prophet.

Zophar continues his theological statement by concluding that if you do everything right by putting

iniquity away from you, then you'll dwell in security —
you'll know that God's on your side.

Job's answer to Zophar is simple, direct and to the
point: *"The tents of robbers are at ease, and those
provoking God secure."*   *Job 12:7*

In other words, if putting iniquity away from you is all
it takes to dwell in security, why are robbers dwelling
free from fear of theft? Why do those who provoke God
not find themselves in the predicament in which Job
found himself?

Again, Job has an incredible and deep understanding of
the nature of God. It is not for thousands of years that
Jesus preached that it rains on the just and the unjust. Yet,
at the same time as the patriarch Abraham, Job understood
that God's mercy is not based upon our actions, but upon
His grace.

Job then chastises the three: *"Would you speak
unrighteously for God, and speak deceitfully for Him?"*
(Job 13:7) Then he continues by saying *"...as one man
mocks another, do you mock Him?"*   *(Verse 9)*

The implication is clear: You guys don't know God at
all, but you presume to speak for Him. How dare you?
Instead of finding out what He's really about, would you
instead teach lies in His name?

Job continues by teaching the men about the nature of
God, whom they obviously have never met:

*"For now You (God) do number my steps; do you not
watch over my sin? My transgression is sealed up in a
bag, and You cover over my iniquity."*   *Job 14:16-17*

Again, Job ends by preaching the Gospel. God, you watch over me — over every step. You know everything I do, and yet you seal my transgression up, and you cover my iniquity.

Right here, Job is trying to explain to his friends that he is not claiming righteousness of his own, but he is claiming the righteousness that comes from surrendering your life to be governed by God. Job describes the relationship by saying God numbers Job's steps. The mental picture is that God is so intimately involved in Job's life that He even knows how many steps Job takes.

But Eliphaz can't stand the idea that Job has just claimed an intimacy with God. In chapter 15, he goes on a rant: who are you to claim to know God? What do you think you know that we don't?

And this is the gist of the reason the Pharisees hated Jesus. Those who have supernatural eyesight are a threat to those who know the words but not the Word.

Here's what Eliphaz says: *"Were you the first man born? Or were you made before the hills? Have you heard the secret counsel of God? And do you limit wisdom to yourself? What do you know that we do not know? Or understand that is not with us? ... What is man that he should be clean? And he born of a woman, that he should be righteous?"*
Job 15:7-9,14

He's saying, just who do you think you are, Job? How can you claim to be clean? You're a man — men can't be clean. How can you claim intimacy with God? You're just like us — you can't know what we don't know.

He can't understand why Job would make the audacious claim that he understands God and that God is intimately involved in Job's life.

This is astounding to all unbelievers. When they hear the voice of a prophet, they laugh and mock, they guffaw and start ranting about how stupid people who claim to know God are.

In chapter 16, Job answers and says *"I have heard many such things. You are all miserable comforters."* (Verse 2)

This is possibly the biggest understatement of the entire book of Job.

He then continues by shaming them: *"I also could speak as you. If your soul were in the place of my soul, I could bind words against you and shake with my head at you."* (Verse 4)

He then says God hadn't done this to him because of his actions — Job doesn't know what His reason is, but it's not because of his sin, which God has forgotten.

When you stop to think about Job's preaching, it is better than that of most of the fine men and women of God who grace the pulpits of our churches today. His preaching, though preached through a body that has been wrung and assaulted, is worthy of the finest preachers in all of history.

In chapter 18, Bildad gets to the root of what the "friends" are trying to say: *"The wicked will die; their light will be put out. They will be scared, hungry, homeless, forgotten. Surely your situation means that you — like they — don't serve God."*

This, in a nutshell, is one of the most popular teachings out there today.

There is a principle in Hinduism called karma. The gist of it is this: when you do something, you will reap it in a later life. If you have a terrible life right now, it's because you did something bad in a previous life. The ultra-modern idea of "instant karma" is that if you do something bad in this life, you'll have troubles later on because of your evil deeds. We can expect the world to teach stupid stuff like "instant karma," but this is one of the most fundamental doctrines of many churches today!

It's all over the TV set! It's all over the popular books!

In chapter 19, Job begins to lose his patience. He says: *"How long will you torment my soul and break me in pieces with words? This ten times you have shamed me; you are not ashamed that you have wronged me. And if indeed I have erred, my error remains with me."*   *Job 19:2-4*

What he's saying is how long will you falsely accuse me? Why are you not ashamed at what you're doing? He later asks them why they seek to magnify themselves against him.

Again, in their actions, we see one of the most popular doctrines that is in practice today. If many Christians see a Christian they respect saying or doing something of which they don't approve, they secretly glory that the person they respected was caught sinning.

They tend to shake their heads at the false accusations of the friends of Job, but in their hearts, many are guilty of the same thing — at least Job's friends were honest enough to come right out and accuse Job. Many today are so cowardly that they accuse people in their hearts so they can feel good about their own lives. This is what Paul was referring to when he said, *"but they measuring themselves by themselves, and comparing themselves among themselves, are not wise."*   *2 Corinthians 10:12*

Job again concludes his response by trying to communicate that the righteousness he claims does not stem from himself:

"For I know that my Redeemer is living, and He shall rise on the earth at the last; and even after they corrupt my skin, yet this: In my flesh I shall see God, whom I shall see for myself, and my eyes shall behold..."   Job 19:25-27

He first says he's justified by his Redeemer, who's alive.

Then he claims that, after he's dead and buried, he shall see God with his own eyes. This the earliest reference to a belief in the resurrection that we have in the Bible.

But more importantly, Job is claiming that his reward is AFTER DEATH, not in this life — his hope is not that he'll reap good things in this life for his righteousness! That's why, when he lost everything, he refused to curse God! He understood that the good things that happened to him were not a result of his righteousness — they were simply blessings. They were undeserved gifts from God! The reward Job is looking for will come after death!

This, partner, is supernatural eyesight in action! In the midst of the most vicious assault against his integrity recorded in the Bible, Job has the strength of conviction to never waver from his understanding of God's truth.

This understanding is obviously gleaned from a highly personal and profound relationship with God.

Zophar can't stand it. In chapter 20, he says that earthly punishment is the reward of the wicked.

He's saying the wicked live in fun and good times for a while. They're revered for a while, but eventually, his wickedness will catch up to him, and he has to pay the piper, so to speak. In effect, Job, this is what's happening to you, he says. He ends by saying this:

"The increase of his house shall depart (from the wicked man), flowing away in the day of (God)'s wrath. This is the evil man's portion from God and the inheritance of his word from God." Job 20:28-29

The difference between what Job is saying and what the accusers who call themselves his friends are saying is small to the natural eye. Both are apparently standing up for God and standing up for God's holiness.

Job's "friends" are even predicting that those who don't serve God can expect misery when their evil deeds catch up to them.

But Job's vision with supernatural eyesight sees right through the dissimulation of the accusers and gets right to the heart of the doctrinal issues they can't seem to grasp.

Job warns the men to listen closely, afterward they can mock if they want.

"Why do the wicked live? They grow old, and become mighty in power. Their seed is established with them before their face, and their offspring before their eyes. Their houses are in peace, without fear, nor is God's rod upon them. His bull mates and does not fail; his cow calves and does not miscarry. ... They lift up voice at the timbrel and lyre, and rejoice at the sound of the flute. They spend their days in good, and in a moment go down to Sheol (hell). And they say to God, Depart from us, for we do not desire the knowledge of Your ways — what is the Almighty, that we should serve Him? And what do we profit if we entreat Him?" Job 21:7-15

Job is saying to Zophar, If your point is true, why do the wicked seem to never pay for their sins in this life? Why do they prosper, make merry, reject God and die? The rich and the poor both live and die. They're buried and the worms eat both of them.

Eliphaz answers and asks a simple question: how can a man be useful to God? Does God even care that you're righteous, Job? You've been wicked. Surely you robbed; surely you stole. Maybe you withheld water from the needy. Maybe you sent a widow away. You did something. In fact, he says in verse 12, you do whatever you want because you believe God is far away and He doesn't see what you do.

At this point, the accusation of the "friends" toward Job are getting more pointed and personal. At every juncture, Job has claimed righteousness, and now they're dispensing with all the politeness and directly accusing him.

In verse 18, Eliphaz claims that the wicked are cut down and fire eats his wealth — he pays his price in this life, and that's exactly what's happening to you, Job! Fire ate your wealth, therefore you must be wicked.

He says, hey, repent, come to intimately know God, and he will restore your health and wealth! Indeed, he gets right to the crux of his point in chapter 22, verse 25: *"Yea, the Almighty shall be your gold and silver, a tower to you* (Remember, Eliphaz's name means 'God of gold'). *For then you will delight over the Almighty, and you will lift up your face to God. You shall make your prayer to him, and he will hear you; and you shall pay your vows. You shall also decide a thing, and it will stand for you; and light shall shine on your ways."*
Job 22:25-28

But Job — using the supernatural eyesight he has gleaned through a tremendous relationship with God — sees right through it.

In chapter 23, verses 11 to 12, he says, *"my foot has held fast in His steps. I have not departed the command of His lips. I treasured His words more than riches."*

Then, in Chapter 24, verse 19, he reiterates that Sheol (hell) is for the unrighteous. His understanding (and again the first time this belief is elucidated in the Bible) is that the sinner's reward is after death — even though they prosper on this earth.

The wisdom of Job is profound in this regard.

Many people read the book of Job and see only the most cursory details of the book — the conversation between God, who is pleased with Job's faithfulness and the devil, who wishes to tempt Job. But the deeper teaching of this incredible book is that Job is a man of incredible depth in the understanding of the nature of God. He has supernatural eyesight — he sees into the spirit realm and understands the deep things of God.

In chapter 25, Bildad repeats his question: how can a man be justified with God? How can a man born of a woman be pure? Even the moon and the stars are not pure in His eyes, Bildad says.

In chapter 26, Job finally says he's had enough. He lays it out for them in a way hopefully even they can't misconstrue:

"The departed spirits writhe from beneath the waters — sheol is naked before (God); the pit has no covering." (verse 5)

"As God lives, He has taken away my judgment. As long as the spirit of God is in my nostrils, my lips won't speak wickedness; my tongue won't lie... I won't retract my integrity because it comes from God, not from me!" (paraphrase of Ch. 27, vv 5-6)

He continues by saying let my enemy become like the world, because he has no hope when he dies.

In verse 19, he says *"The wicked lies down, but he is not gathered!"*

This is fascinating, because in the patriarch narratives, we always learn that the patriarchs, when they die, are "gathered to their fathers." In the New Testament, Jesus states that the patriarchs are not dead, because God is the God of the living. Job here says that the wicked die, but they are not gathered as the patriarchs were — their reward is after they die!

Who is Job, and where did he come up with such profound wisdom?

The Bible does not tell us.

But the fact is, Job lived at a time at least four hundred years before Moses ever set pen to paper to compose the first five books of the Bible. With no written revelation to guide him, Job came to his profound understanding of God and the coming Messiah without the Scriptures that tell us what He's all about.

There have been many suggestions made by various people throughout the ages as to where Job came up with such profound insight into the Gospel thousands of years before John the Baptist and the advent of Jesus Christ.

Some have suggested that, because *"The heavens declare the glory of God; and the firmament sheweth his handywork" (Psalms 19:1)*, that God declared His Word to Job through a message literally written in the stars.

That very well could be the answer. Or it could be something else. Job was, after all, only a very few generations removed from Noah, the man God chose to spare on the ark during the flood that killed everyone else.

It could be that Job's family passed down the understanding of the Gospel to him, being so few generations removed from the righteous Noah.

Whatever its source, we can tell some very profound things from Job's answers to the accusers who called themselves his friends:

- Job had a very personal relationship with God — a relationship that both stemmed from his understanding of God (his supernatural eyesight) and also engendered his supernatural eyesight

- Job held no illusions that he was sin-free; instead, he understood that his righteousness was based upon God's mercy — another insight that was thousands of years before its time.

As we continue learning the keys to supernatural eyesight, the wisdom of Job reminds us that there is a singular relationship between the eyesight into the spiritual things of God and the relationship that results from it.

Supernatural eyesight comes from a relationship with God — and supernatural eyesight that comes from that relationship will draw you ever more deeply into the presence of God.

One leads to the other, and one cannot survive in your life without the other.

If you see into the spirit, you'll be consumed with a desire to delve even deeper, to know more. The more you know, the more you'll want to know and, just as Job, you'll find yourself knowing more and more, the revelation literally unpeeling layer by layer as you deepen your relationship with God.

Isaiah worded it like this:

"Whom shall he teach knowledge? and whom shall he make to understand doctrine? them that are weaned from the milk, and drawn from the breasts. For precept must be upon precept, precept upon precept; line upon line, line upon line; here a little, and there a little:" Isaiah 28:9-10

CHAPTER 3

WHAT WAS THE SECRET OF NOAH, ABRAHAM, JACOB AND JOSEPH?

God has, throughout the history of mankind, sought to have relationships with men.

But by the time of Noah, mankind had become so corrupt that God had only one man to have a relationship with.

Not only that, but mankind had corrupted themselves and were in danger of corrupting the entire earth with their sin:

"And Jehovah saw that the evil of man was great on the earth, and every imagination of the thought of his heart was only evil all the day long. ... The earth also was corrupt before God. And the earth was filled with violence. And God looked upon the earth, and behold, it was corrupt; for all flesh had corrupted his way on the earth. And God said unto Noah, The end of all flesh is come before me; for the earth is filled with violence through them; and, behold, I will destroy them with the earth."
Genesis 6:5, 11-13, (Direct translation from Hebrew)

From that time to this, the wickedness of mankind has not again reached such a level where it threatened to corrupt the very earth.

The sinners who were inhabiting the earth had more than 900 years of life each in which to think up new ways to sin.

The oldest man recorded in the Bible was Methusaleh, who lived 969 years. But that's just the oldest man *recorded*. Methusaleh died the year of the flood; who knows how long he might have lived if the flood had not come? Since the Bible only goes into great detail about the men in the line of Noah, it's possible that people who were not in that line lived even longer than Methusaleh and we just don't know about it because it's not recorded for our benefit.

In any case, we know that many of the men had at least 900 years to dream up new and devious ways to disobey the words of God.

As God looked over the earth, the Bible says He "repented" that he made man. But that word is difficult to translate into English. The actual Hebrew word, "Mhanf" means to be sigh or breathe heavily, as in to be brought to great sorrow.

The wickedness of mankind, which God had created — unlike any of the animals — with the ability to either worship or sin, brought Him to great sorrow.

As God is planning to destroy the earth — meaning specifically the inhabitants of it — he finds one man who is righteous.

The Bible says this: *"And Noah found grace in the eyes of Jehovah. These are the generations of Noah. Noah, a righteous man, had been perfected among his family — Noah walked with God."*

Genesis 6:8-9

This tiny snippet of Scripture tells us so much about Noah.

Noah was righteous — because, like Job, he had "found grace" in the eyes of God.

In the second chapter, we discussed Job, who maintained that he was righteous not by his own virtue, but by virtue of a redeemer who would forgive his sins and raise him up in the last day.

Here we also see that Noah was a man depending on grace, not the righteousness that comes by works.

But not only was he full of grace, he "walked with God."

In other words, Noah *spent time* with God. He did not just pray a prayer every once in awhile. He did not claim to be a servant of God and then just go on about the rest of his life following his own desires.

Noah was a man whose life revolved around God.

Many people see a phrase like "walking with God" and they envision some super-spiritual person with their heads in the clouds…

But walking with God is as simple as doing what Noah later demonstrates: it's simply spending time with God, listening to Him and obeying what He says.

One of the keys to spiritual eyesight is understanding that God is the source of our very lives; our walk with Him must be based not on some super-spiritual, pie-in-the-sky mumbo-jumbo. Instead, our walk must be based on a very real, very down-to-earth concept: He talks, we listen and obey.

As God speaks to Noah, some very profound insights into Noah's relationship with God come to light:

- God reveals to Noah His plan

- God reveals why He's doing what He's doing

- God gives him instructions

- Noah obeys without question

Pay close attention, because this is of utmost importance.

First, God reveals His plan to the righteous man: *"And God said to Noah, the end of all flesh has come before Me...And behold, I will destroy them along with the earth ... And behold, I, even I, am bringing a flood of waters on the earth in order to destroy all flesh in which is the breath of life from under the heavens. Everything which is on the earth shall die."*   *Genesis 6:13, 17*

The Bible tells us a profound truth in Amos: *"Surely the Lord GOD will do nothing, but he revealeth his secret unto his servants the prophets."*   *Amos 3:7*

A prophet is simply someone who is inspired by God.

Certainly Noah, then, could be counted as a prophet.

God reveals His plan to the prophet, and then God explains WHY He's doing it: *"for the earth is filled with violence through them."*   *Genesis 6:13*

Noah had God-given insight (you might say spiritual eyesight) into the root cause of the problem: the earth was filled with violence through the actions of the sinful men who inhabited it.

Once God had given His prophet the insight into the root cause of the problem and God's plan to take care of the problem, He instructs the prophet on what to do:

"Make an ark of cyprus timbers for yourself. You shall make rooms in the ark; and you shall cover it with asphalt inside and out."   *Genesis 6:14*

God gives the prophet specific instructions — not vague concepts, but specific instructions. And the prophet, demonstrating the nature that the Bible says is righteous, immediately goes about to do what the Lord has instructed him to do: *"And Noah did so, according to all that God commanded him, so he did."*   *Genesis 6:22*

After Noah obeys God, God explains to him why He's chosen Noah: *"And Jehovah said to Noah, You and all your house come into the ark, for I have seen you righteous before me in this generation."*   *Genesis 7:1*

Noah had attained a place that many others have sought for and have not found. In Matthew, Jesus speaks about the place most find: *"Not every one that saith unto me, Lord, Lord, shall enter into the kingdom of heaven; but he that doeth the will of my Father which is in heaven. Many will say to me in that day, Lord, Lord, have we not prophesied in thy name? and in thy name have cast out devils? and in thy name done many wonderful works? And then will I profess unto them, I never knew you: depart from me, ye that work iniquity."*   *Matthew 7:21-23*

There are many who ***do the works that accompany righteousness.***

But the works do not make one righteous.

The works follow righteousness. When someone is righteous, God knows them. Jesus claimed to those working works without righteousness, "I don't know you."

But those who *live* righteousness will do the works that are a natural fruit of righteousness.

That's why God tells Noah, "I have seen you righteous."

When someone is righteous, God sees them and knows them. When someone works the works without the righteousness that comes by grace and faith, God does not honor those works.

And in Noah's case, God testified that Noah was both righteous and accepted in the eyes of God.

That's important, because Noah was the single man on the entire face of the earth that God found righteous enough to rescue from the coming destruction.

Noah's three sons were rescued, but according to Genesis 7:1, they were rescued not because of their own righteousness, but because of Noah's.

Remember, all of this stemmed from one simple sentence: "Noah walked with God."

The key to Noah's spiritual eyesight, the key to his righteousness, the key to his very survival, came from the fact that he constructed his entire life around the will of God.

He walked with God in such a profound manner that God found him alone righteous in his generation.

But the New Testament sheds even more light on Noah's understanding of the things of God.

When Peter is instructing the Church in his second letter, he states this: *"And (God) spared not the old world, but saved Noah the eighth person, **a preacher of righteousness…"***
                                                                                                   2 Peter 2:5

Not only was Noah a righteous man in his generation, a man who walked with God, who received revelation knowledge from God and acted on that knowledge, according to the Apostle Peter, Noah also **PREACHED** the righteousness of God to his generation.

This is SUPERNATURAL EYESIGHT in action!

Remember, Noah was a man who had "found grace" in the eyes of God, and that, according to the Bible, made him righteous.

So the righteousness that he was preaching was likely the same righteousness he was practicing!

This shows us a principle of God's Word that is always demonstrated: God does not bring destruction without first sending a prophet — a speaker for the righteousness of God to warn the generation in danger and to preach the righteousness of God.

As you read this book understand that we — you and I — are called to be those voices to this end-time generation.

We are called, like Noah, to see into the supernatural and receive the word from God and publish it to this generation — we are the "preacher of righteousness" today!

Noah, when the flood was over, demonstrated again his keen understanding of God's nature and the reality that his righteousness came through the grace of God: he built an altar to God to thank Him for His salvation.

The result of his supernatural eyesight was that Noah was able to perceive things around him that others likely would not perceive.

"And Noah, a man of the ground, began and planted a vineyard. And he drank from the wine, and was drunk. And he uncovered himself inside his tent. And Ham, the father of Canaan, saw the nakedness of his father, and he told his two brothers outside. And Shem and Japheth took a garment and put it on both their shoulders. And they went backwards and covered the nakedness of their father, their faces backward. And they did not see the nakedness of their father. And Noah awoke from his wine. And he came to know what his younger son had done to him."

Genesis 9:20-24

Through his supernatural understanding, Noah was able to discern that his son had sinned in folly.

Noah's secret was that he, through his diligence and submission to God, was able to see into the supernatural and understand both the nature of God and hear His voice.

After the flood, God told Noah and his offspring to go, fill the earth and replenish it. Noah's offspring did not obey, however — the entire world was gathered near the place called Babel (later Babylon, in modern-day Iraq).

Not only did they not obey God's commandment, the Bible says they schemed out ways to avoid obeying it. When the population of Babel became too great, the men of the city decided to build a tower for an express purpose:

*"And they said, 'Come, let us build for ourselves a city, and a tower whose top will reach into the heavens, and let us make for ourselves a name, **lest we be scattered abroad over the face of the whole earth.'"***   *Genesis 11:4*

Their goal was to fashion a way in which they could ignore the commandment of God and stay in one geographic region of the planet.

Of course, we all know the story. God confounded their language, and they scattered anyway.

Only a very few generations later, a man in the same region of Babel in a city named Ur had a family and moved to Haran (in modern-day Syria). The man, Terah, had a son named Abram.

"And Jehovah said to Abram, Go out from your land, and from your kindred, and from your father's house, to the land which I will show you. And I will make of you a great nation. And I will bless you and make your name great; and you will be a blessing. And I will bless those who bless you, and curse the one despising you. And in you shall all the families of the earth be blessed."

Genesis 12:1-3

The Bible says that many are called, but few are chosen.

Abram was called, but it was up to him to obey — God delivered a commandment to him, and then explained to him the benefits if he chose to obey God.

The Bible shows us that, almost immediately, Abram's life was changed — he became a man who heard and obeyed God, a man of integrity.

He became a man of God, a man who follows where God leads.

In fact, as soon as he began following God, Abram began to exhibit one of the key attributes of those who have supernatural eyesight: he became a natural leader.

This is often overlooked, and yet it is one of the most important attributes of someone who is a believer: those who become followers of God become leaders of men.

They become leaders not because they know how to command, but because they lead by example. Remember in the first chapter, I explained how Jesus never did a work except He first saw His Father do it. God's kind of leadership is that He leads by example.

He doesn't ask us to do anything He hasn't first done.

So when the people of God become followers of Him and begin to see with supernatural eyesight into His nature and His mysteries, they become leaders by example as they follow His lead.

In fact, Abram immediately demonstrates this kind of leadership after God calls him out of Haran:

"And Abram went out, even as Jehovah had spoken to him. And Lot went with him. And Abram was seventy-five years old when he departed from Haran. And Abram took his wife Sarai, and his brother's son, Lot, and all their substance that they had gathered, and the persons they had gained in Haran. And they went out to go into the land of Canaan."   *Genesis 12:4-5*

Abram follows God's lead, and Lot follows Abram.

Immediately, the characteristics of leadership were on Abram because he had obeyed God and gained a new insight — a supernatural eyesight. Abram led because he was following God.

It's important to remember, though, that seeing and hearing the things of God is just like natural eyesight — you must continue looking and listening to develop your hearing and sight. A baby can see, but can't discern between the sights.

Abram, who had been the son of an idol worshiper, was radically changed by his encounter with God, and he wasn't about to let that experience stagnate and sit in his life.

How many times do Christians have an experience with God and let that experience drive them for the rest of their lives, never seeking a deeper revelation, never seeking a deeper relationship. They are content instead to feed off of yesterday's manna, glorying in experiences of the past.

But Abram seemed to understand that God is a God of today — that today is when He wants us to seek Him, to pray, meditate and worship.

As soon as Abram gets into the land of Canaan, God appears to him again: *"And Jehovah appeared to Abram and said, 'I will give this land to your seed.' And he built an altar there to Jehovah, who appeared to him."*

Genesis 12:7

Just as Noah had a few generations earlier, Abram had an encounter with God and immediately built an altar to worship God and deepen both his relationship with God and his understanding of God.

This is one of the attributes of those who have supernatural eyesight — their constant goal is to see more, to hear more, to enter a deeper relationship with God than they were in yesterday.

After a short time in Egypt, Abram again went back to Canaan, where God had called him, and: *"Abram called on the name of Jehovah there."* *Genesis 13:4*

What the Bible is painting is a picture of a man whose life is dedicated to prayer — it seems everywhere he goes,

Abram is praying, building an altar or calling on the name of God.

But the first true test of Abram's understanding of God, His call and His promises comes in the eighth verse — a passage of Scripture that shows Abram had a profound understanding of both the promises of God and the nature of God.

Abram and Lot had become rich in livestock, and their herdsmen were having strife because the livestock were too numerous for the land to support.

"And Abram said to Lot, Please let there be no strife between me and you, and between my herdsmen and your herdsmen, for we are men, brothers. Is not all the land before you? Please separate from me. If you go to the left, then I will go to the right. Or if you go to the right, then I will go to the left."   *Genesis 13:8-9*

Now, remember that God had promised ALL the land to Abram, not to Lot. Abram could have thrown that up in Lot's face and said something along the lines of, "Hey, God gave this land to me, not you. Take your stingy herdsmen and find yourself someplace else to graze."

But the profound impact of God on the life and nature of Abram was evident in the way he handled the situation — he gave Lot his choice of the best land.

Abram didn't tell Lot what land he could have; he believed God's promise and trusted that God would fulfill the promise, no matter what Lot did. So Abram told Lot to take whatever land he wanted, and Abram would take the leftovers.

I can't stress enough how important this lesson from Abram's life is.

CHAPTER 3: WHAT WAS THE SECRET OF NOAH, ABRAHAM, JACOB AND JOSEPH?

He had received the promise from God, but he refused to seize it outside of God's timing! God had promised him the land, but, through an incredible insight into the spirit, he understood that if God had promised it, God was able to deliver what He had promised.

And though God had promised the land to Abram, he gave Lot the choice of the best land because he understood that God would not let anyone stand in the way of fulfilling a promise!

In the very next chapter, Abram again demonstrates that he has a profound understanding of the promises of God — and that the hand of man is powerless to deliver or constrain what God has promised.

Lot was captured in a tremendous battle, and Abram pursued and defeated the army that had enslaved Lot. On his way back, the king of Sodom came out with an enticing offer for Abram:

"Give me the persons and take the goods for yourself."
Genesis 14:21

The offer is that Abram could, in one fell swoop, become fabulously wealthy in goods — likely gold, silver, weapons and all sorts of the booty that comes from winning a tremendous battle. The king of Sodom offers to let Abram keep all the treasure.

But Abram, who is a man of prayer and who, like Noah, walks with God, wants nothing to do with the king of Sodom's offer:

"And Abram said to the king of Sodom, I have lifted up my hand to Jehovah, the most high God, the possessor of heaven and earth, that I will not take from all that is

53

*yours, from a thread to a shoe-latchet, and that you may
not say, I have made Abram rich. Nothing for me; only
what the young men have eaten, and the portion of the
men who went with me...let them take their portion."*

Genesis 14:22-24

This, again, is supernatural eyesight in action in the life
of Abram. He, by the power of God's action in his life, is
able to discern that the king of Sodom has less-than-
honorable motives in offering the riches to Abram, and he
won't stand for anyone trying to claim the glory that
rightly belongs to God!

God has promised Abram incredible blessings, and
Abram won't let the king of Sodom claim that he, not
God, had made Abram rich.

As you may have been able to tell up to this point,
discernment is a byproduct of seeing in the supernatural
— of having an intimate relationship with God.

Some today would doubtlessly accept the offer of the
king of Sodom, and then praise God that His word had
been fulfilled through the king of Sodom.

But Abram understood — through his relationship
with God — that the hand of man was not what would
be Abram's blessing; instead, it would be a
supernatural blessing. God was going to bless Abram
by His own hand, not through the generosity of a king
with ulterior motives.

This is why supernatural eyesight is that which
maintains focus on the things of God! Jesus said if your
eyes are on both God and money, your entire body will be
full of darkness. Like the lioness focusing on her prey,
your eyes must be focused on the things of God — and

not be distracted by the deceitfulness of the world's goals. Abram knew wealth was coming his way, but he did not let that distract him from the fact that it was GOD who was going to make it happen. His eyes were firmly focused on God and his goal was to glorify God through the fulfillment of the promises.

But Abram, who is called the "father of faith," has more lessons than just this to teach us about supernatural eyesight.

His life serves as a textbook, so to speak, about exactly how God desires to have a relationship with man.

After he has rejected the seditious offer of the king of Sodom, Abram has a vision, during which he asks God exactly *how* the promises He made to him will be fulfilled. This not only demonstrates that God wants a back-and-forth relationship with us, it also shows that God is more than willing to answer our questions if only we have *ears to hear*.

"After these things the word of Jehovah came to Abram in a vision, saying, Do not fear, Abram; I am your shield, your reward will increase greatly. And Abram said, Lord Jehovah, what will You give to me, since I am going childless ... behold! You have given no seed to me; and lo, the son of my house is inheriting of me. And behold! The word of Jehovah came to him saying, this one shall not be your heir. But he that shall come forth out of your own bowels shall be your heir. And he brought him outside and said, Look now at the heavens and count the stars, if you are able to count them. And he said to him, so shall your seed be. And he believed in Jehovah. And He counted it to him for righteousness." Genesis 15:1-8

Abram, in the vision, wanted to know exactly how God was going to fulfill the promise He had made to him earlier in Haran.

One of the keys to seeing with supernatural eyesight is to simply be honest with God.

So many today are superstitiously afraid that if they even ask God a question, God will be angry with them and destroy them.

But God is not looking for religiously perfect people — He is looking for people who will be honest with Him. Abram had a question, and he was not afraid to ask it!

Even Jesus, when he was about to suffer crucifixion, was brutally honest with His Father:

*"And he went forward a little, and fell on the ground, and prayed that, if it were possible, the hour might pass from him. And he said, Abba, Father, **all things are possible unto thee**; take away this cup from me: nevertheless not what I will, but what thou wilt."*
Mark 14:35-36

Racked with the knowledge that His passion was upon Him, Jesus cried out in stark honesty to God: God, I would like a way out of this fate, if it's possible! He cried out to God that all things are possible — You can think of another way to accomplish this if You want to! But then He demonstrates another aspect of supernatural eyesight — he commits Himself to accomplish God's will, even though everything in Him wants to find some other way to do it.

Just as for Abram, it would have been easier to accomplish God's will by letting the king of Sodom bless him, it would have been easier for Jesus at that moment to let God's will come about in some other way. But Jesus resolved within Himself to do God's will anyway.

But the sheer, stark honesty of the prayer of Jesus to His Father serves as an example to us — God doesn't want us to try to pray what we think He wants to hear from us.

Instead, He wants us to pray what's in our hearts. God wants to hear from you, not from the religion you've learned to use to disguise yourself.

So when Abram asked God how He would fulfill His promise, it shows that he had an understanding of that: God wasn't looking for super-spiritual prayers from Abram. He was looking for Abram to talk to Him.

Simply speaking, if you've ever been to one of my meetings, you've likely heard me talking about taking the mask off.

The mask is the religion in which we disguise our true selves. We think God wants us to pray a certain way, so we hide ourselves under the mask of that prayer. We think God wants us to think a certain way, so we deny what we're really thinking and try to act as if we're thinking the way God wants us to think.

But all God wants from us is the same He wanted from Abram: take the mask off. Be honest and come to Him as yourself, not as yourself coated in religion and the famous catch-phrases of religion that make you feel super spiritual.

One thing is true about almost all masks — when you're wearing them, it's difficult to see — because the eyeholes are trying to disguise you.

You can never operate in supernatural eyesight until you are willing to cast aside all the vain religious psychobabble and just come to God as a human being who has fears, needs, desires and sometimes a lack of faith.

Did you know that the Bible calls Abraham a prophet?

In Genesis 20:7, God says explicitly, *"for he is a prophet."*

But before that explicit statement, the Bible implies that Abram is a prophet, when, after his conversation with God, his vision turns dark:

"And it happened as the sun was setting, and a deep sleep fell on Abram, and behold, a terror of great darkness falling on him! And He said to Abram, You must surely know that your seed shall be an alien in a land not theirs; and they shall serve them. And they shall afflict them four hundred years; and I also will judge that nation whom they shall serve; and afterward, they shall come out with great substance. And you shall come to your fathers in peace. You shall be buried in a good old age. And in the fourth generation they shall come here again; for the iniquity of the Amorites is not yet full."

Genesis 15:12-16

God shows Abram incredible things in the Spirit. He shows him of the upcoming 400 years of bondage in Egypt. He shows him of his own longevity. He shows him of the iniquity and the eventual judgment of the Amorites.

These visions were all a natural man — Abram — seeing into the supernatural by the power of the living God.

There was nothing that Abram did to specially prepare himself for this incredible visitation from the Lord. He did not pray a special prayer, fast a special fast or walk a dozen miles. He simply made himself available to God and when God moved upon him, Abram saw into the spirit world supernaturally and discerned the things to come as God showed them to him.

But Abram is only in the very beginning of his supernatural eyesight — his relationship with God was destined to grow deeper and more profound, and God increased the clarity of Abram's vision as Abram followed Him.

In Genesis 18:1, we find Abraham by the oaks of Mamre (vigor). It's a hot day, and Abraham is sitting in the door of his tent.

Verse one tells us God appeared to him there.

Abraham doesn't notice three men walk up to him. Instead, he looked up and they were suddenly there: "And he lifted up his eyes and looked; and behold, three men were standing by him."   *Verse 3*

Now Abraham does an interesting thing.

He runs out to meet them, and he bows himself to the ground.

He calls them "my Lord" or אֲדֹנָי ;(Adonai). The form of the word Abraham uses is exclusively used in reference to God. So he sees these three men and calls them Lord, meaning God.

Abraham entreats the Lord to stay a bit, wash his feet, rest under the tree and eat a bit of bread before He continues on His way, because *"this is why you have passed over to Your servant."*   *Genesis 18:5*

It's interesting to parallel this with the New Testament, where Jesus washes the feet of the disciples. It was a sign of hospitality, as sandals did little to keep the grime of the sand and dirt off the feet of travelers.

In verses 9 and 10, God again reiterates His promise to Abram:

"And they said to him, Where is your wife, Sarah? And he said, See, in the tent. And He said, I will certainly return to you at the time of life; and, behold, a son shall be to your wife Sarah. And Sarah was listening at the entrance to the tent, and it was behind Him."

And though God is reiterating His promise to Abraham, in verse 16, they get into the second part of the men's visit with Abraham. They get up and look toward Sodom. As Abraham accompanies them, *"Jehovah said, Shall I hide from Abraham that which I am doing?"*

Again we see the recurrent theme: God does nothing without first telling His prophets.

In this case, there is little Abraham can do to warn the inhabitants, but they have had a righteous man (Lot) in their midst for quite some time.

In verse 19, God gives an incredible endorsement of Abraham that is often overlooked: *"For I have known him."*

This is the crux of the difference between those who know the words and those who know the Word.

Abraham is known by God because he has made himself completely available to God. He has made himself God's servant, totally trusting in Him and believing that He will accomplish His promises by supernatural means.

God continues His almost casual conversation with Abraham: *"The cry of Sodom and Gomorrah is great, and their sin is exceedingly heavy. I will go down and see if they have at all done according to the cry coming to Me. And if not, I will know."* Genesis 18:20

Those who have a deep relationship with God are privy to His doings — God speaks to them and gives them an indication of what He's about to do. We saw it earlier in the case of Noah, and now we see it in the life of Abraham. God is preparing to do a great deal of destruction, but first He lets His prophet know what's going on.

It's also interesting to note that although God has not explicitly stated His intention to destroy the city, Abraham assumes that's God's plan. Abraham, knowing God, perceives that His intentions are to destroy Sodom for the cry of wickedness that has proceeded up from it.

Abraham begins his famous bargaining for the city. He first asks God if He will spare the city if He finds 50 righteous people there because *"Far be it from You to act in this way, to put to death the righteous with the wicked, that the righteous should be as the wicked." 18:25*

Abraham is demonstrating that he had a fundamental grasp of the nature of God. He knew that God is righteous and that He would do no unrighteous thing. Because the sizes of cities in those days was relatively small, 50 people, even though still a prohibitive minority, represented a larger portion of the population than it would today.

So when God agrees to spare the entire population if He finds even this tiny minority of righteous people, Abraham presses his case for 45, 40, 30, 20 and 10.

Again, we must understand the rhetorical nature of God's statement to Abraham in verse 21. He already knew what was going on in Sodom. This conversation was for *Abraham's* benefit, not for God's. It was in this

conversation that God set out the limits of His wrath —
for 10 people, He would spare the entire population.

He is revealing even more of His nature to Abraham —
as Abraham grows in his relationship with God, God
reveals ever more of Himself; Abraham's supernatural
eyesight is that much clearer.

Abraham's secret to supernatural eyesight was simple: he
hid nothing of himself from God, and when God spoke, he
listened and believed.

But if you want to know about supernatural eyesight,
an even more profound and progressive lesson is in the
life of the grandson of Abraham — a man who started
out life struggling with flesh and blood and ended up
life having prevailed with men and with God. Jacob
became a man who through his son subjugated the
mightiest nation on earth.

Jacob's life started out as a mortal struggle against his
own brother:

*"And (Rebekah's) sons struggled together within her.
And she said, if this is right, why am I this way? And
she went to ask Jehovah. And Jehovah said to her, Two
nations are in your womb; yea, two peoples shall break
from your body. And one people shall be stronger
than the other people; and the elder shall serve
the younger."*
Genesis 25:22-23

The word translated as "struggled" is much more
graphic than the English word. It means to crack in
pieces, either literally or figuratively, to break, bruise,
crush or oppress.

Rebekah's sons were not just "struggling." They were in an all-out, knock-down, drag-out fight.

But their fight is not one that will end quickly.

As Rebekah goes to give birth, the fight is still going on; Jacob comes out with his hand holding onto his brother's heel — refusing to give up the fight.

But his perseverance earns him a less-than-honorable name.

His parents name him Jacob אַיְעֲקֹב, which means "heel-catcher."

Imagine being stuck with a name like that all your life. Everywhere you went, people would know that your parents had named you for grabbing a heel, for supplanting your brother.

The name in large part proved true for the early part of Jacob's life. In a moment of weakness, he convinces his brother to sell his birthright to him for the price of a bowl of lentil soup (from which Esau got his nickname, Edom, because of the color of the lentils, red).

In addition, Jacob (the heel-grabber) disguises himself to receive the blessing that was intended for his brother.

But after his father's death, Jacob went to Haran to seek a wife from the family of his mother, whose brother, Laban, was still there.

It's on the way there that Jacob has what we in the modern world would call a "salvation moment."

In Genesis 28:12-13, Jacob falls asleep and has a dream: "*Behold, a ladder was placed on the earth, its top reaching to the heavens. And, behold, the angels of God were going up and going down on it! And, behold, Jehovah stood above it and said, I am Jehovah the God of your father Abraham, and the God of Isaac; the land on which you are lying, I will give it to you and your seed."*

This is the beginning of a long and incredible transformation of the heel-catcher.

His story and his journey are inspirational to us because Jacob is more like us than many of the other heroes of the Bible; he is a petty man who's looking out for Number One above all else.

But when the transformation of his life begins, he starts to see with supernatural eyesight into the deep things of God, and his entire life transforms to the point that for the rest of time, the people of God will be called by his name!

In verse 20 of the same chapter, Jacob makes a vow to God:

"If God is with me and keeps me ... and I return in peace .. then Jehovah shall be my God, and all which You shall give to me, I will tithe the tenth to You."

This is the same sort of thing that happened to Abram. Jacob hears the promise and the call of God, he believes the word of God and he acts on the calling.

It is a fundamental mile marker in the life of any person of faith: we must hear the call of God. We must believe it. We must act on it.

And immediately Jacob's character begins to change — he becomes, instead of a "heel-grabber," a man of integrity.

He goes, and keeping his word even when his uncle deals unrighteously with him, he serves him for his two daughters and the children they bear to him in Laban's household.

During that time, God blesses Laban tremendously because of Jacob — both fulfilling His promise to Abraham to bless those who bless him, and fulfilling His promise to Jacob.

And Jacob, who started out as a bad sort, has matured to the point that he, like Abraham before him, has supernatural eyesight into the promises of God, and understands that God has promised to bless him and nothing can stop that blessing.

Laban will do almost anything to keep Jacob in his household and, much like the king of Sodom, he offers to make Jacob rich by giving him an estate.

But in Genesis 30:31, Jacob refuses to be increased through the gift of a man: *"You shall not give me anything. If you will do this thing for me, I will remain."* And starting in verse 32, he offers to take the spotted, flecked and striped sheep and the black sheep, leaving the better sheep for Laban in return for his labor. Jacob doesn't want any gift. He wants to work for any goods he receives from men.

He demonstrates that he, like Abraham, profoundly understands the nature of God's promises to him — it won't be by the hand of man that God blesses him.

"And my righteousness shall testify for me in the day to come."   *Genesis 30:32*

He, like Abraham, was content to take the leftovers and give the better blessings to those around him, knowing that God would bring about his blessing in due time. Indeed,

he seems to have innately understood what was later written in the Psalms: *"Wait on the Lord: be of good courage, and he shall strengthen thine heart: wait, I say, on the Lord."*
Psalm 27:14

But as he's leaving the land of Haran for Canaan at the command of God, Jacob demonstrates that he has truly gained an incredible insight into the nature of God and his role in God's plan.

God has commanded him to go, but he fears his brother Esau, who, years earlier, had wanted him dead. Going back he might face a battle and even death at the hands of Esau.

He, as Abraham before him, and as Jesus later, does not try to disguise his fear as he goes before God in prayer:

"I am not worthy of all the mercies and all the truth which You have done for Your servant ... deliver me ... from the hand ... of Esau, for I fear him."
Genesis 32:9-11

Again, he doesn't try to couch his prayer in religious language of false faith or super-piety. Instead, he takes the mask off and pours out his heart to the One from whom he knows his blessings flow. This is clearly a different man from the one who bought his brother's birthright and supplanted his blessing.

Jacob fears so much that he divides his family up into two branches and sends streams of gifts to Esau to try to "soften him up," so to speak.

But the evidence of God's supernatural eyesight in Jacob's life is that, as much as he fears the death he's certain he's facing, HE DOES NOT TURN BACK.

God had told him to go back to the land of his father, and Jacob had made a vow to God to be His servant. As much as he feared, he knew enough about God to determine that, even if it cost him his life, he would not disobey the living God who had blessed him so much and made such incredible promises to him.

This is one of the most powerful aspects of supernatural eyesight: sticking to what God has told you even when everything in the natural seems to suggest disaster is on its way!

Starting in verse 24 of the 32nd chapter of Genesis, Jacob gets into his famous wrestling match with the "man." I put "man" in quotes because the "man" appears to be a man, but is anything but; he is supernatural.

Jacob and the "man" wrestle hard enough to kick up a cloud of dust, because the Hebrew word translated "wrestle" actually literally means to wrestle hard enough to raise a cloud of dust.

This was no mamby-pamby wrestling match. It was an all-out, winner-take all fight! But Jacob, who had been wrestling since he was in his mother's womb, was no pushover — he wrestled the "man" through the night, and the "man" saw that he was not able to overcome Jacob, so he violently struck the hip of Jacob, dislocating it. Despite the incredible pain this must have caused him, Jacob continues to prevail in the wrestling match until the day is at hand. The man tells Jacob to let him go, because the day is approaching. But Jacob, realizing that this is no man —

again exhibiting his discernment that comes with supernatural eyesight — won't let the "man" go unless he blesses Jacob.

This is an incredible turning point in Jacob's life.

He got the name "heel-catcher" because he LOST the wrestling match in his mother's womb.

But now, he loses the name "heel-catcher" because he WON the wrestling match with the "man." So instead of the "heel-catcher," Jacob becomes Israel — which means "he will rule (as) God."

And once he talks with the "man," Jacob understands who the "man" is and names the place Peniel the (face of God) because, *"I saw God face-to-face and my life is preserved."*
Genesis 32:30

Again Jacob demonstrates that he has a profound understanding of the nature of God. He understands that God has been there with him all night, and he has lived to tell the tale, which means God has had tremendous mercy on him.

He seems to innately understand what God later explained explicitly to Moses: *"And he said, Thou canst not see my face: for there shall no man see me, and live."*
Exodus 33:20

The Bible does not tell us how God enacted his mercy on Jacob — whether he hid enough of his face to keep Jacob alive, or whether he simply had mercy. In any case, Jacob, through the supernatural eyesight he has gained by his profound relationship with God, understands that he has done something that should not have left him alive, and yet he has lived.

The transformation of Jacob to Israel is complete.

He has, as the Christian today, gone from a "heel-grabber"
to a man who "will rule as God."

And along the way, he has gained an incredible
supernatural eyesight — an incredible perception into the
spiritual world based upon his profoundly deep
relationship with God.

The transformation is one we all must go through —
from sinner to saint, not by the power of our own
abilities, but by the grace of a God who desires to have
an intimate relationship with us. And, much as Jacob,
we along the way must develop an insight into God's
Word and His nature that is based upon our deepening
relationship with Him.

Israel's son, Joseph, is the favorite son of the favorite
wife of Israel. He spends time with his father, gaining
valuable insight into his father's relationship with God and
into his character.

His brothers, however, resent him, and we all know the
familiar story — they sell him into slavery on a caravan
headed for Egypt.

Joseph had a tremendous insight into God's character —
and that insight guided him to the top place in the world's
most powerful nation.

His first assignment as a slave was in the house of a
man named Potiphar. He ended up being in charge of all
of Potiphar's affairs, to the point that the Bible says
Potiphar *"did not know anything that he had, except the
bread that he was eating."*   *Genesis 39:6*

The story is painfully familiar. Potiphar's wife, who was attracted by Joseph, who was "beautiful in form and beautiful in appearance," sought to get him to have an illicit sex affair with her.

Joseph immediately demonstrates a supernatural understanding that will only increase over time:

"Behold, my master does not know what is in the house with me, and all that he owns he has given into my hand. No one in the house is greater than I, and he has not withheld anything from me except you, because you are his wife. And how should I do this great evil and sin against God?"

Genesis 39:8-9

Joseph understands that the sin he would commit by committing adultery with Potiphar's wife would be a sin against God above all. His concern is for Potiphar in the immediate, but his ultimate concern is that it would damage his relationship with God to commit such a sin.

In the midst of probably the second-most stressful moment of his life, Joseph is not thinking of the physical consequences of his actions — he's thinking first of God and how it will affect his relationship with God.

Joseph, who's later thrown into prison after the wife falsely accuses him of making unwanted advances, continues to grow in supernatural eyesight.

In the prison, his relationship with God is so profound that the warden puts him over the entire prison, which is a testimony to the blessings of God that were on Joseph's life. After all, the leader of the prison could be executed if a major disaster happened under his stewardship. At the very least, he could lose his freedom and be imprisoned with those he was formerly over.

For him to put that kind of trust into the hands of a foreigner who was a slave and then imprisoned was tremendous indeed — another testimony of the action of God in the life of Joseph.

But the most impressive example of the insight God had granted Joseph is about to happen: Pharaoh's cup-bearer and his baker are apparently both accused of a crime. Pharaoh orders them imprisoned apparently until he can figure out which of them is guilty.

Potiphar assigns Joseph to care for the two high-level prisoners while they're in the prison.

Both men have a dream, and they come to Joseph because they're upset by the dreams.

In Genesis 40:8, Joseph demonstrates that he has a powerful insight into the nature of the spirit realm. He tells the cup bearer and the baker, *"do not interpretations belong to God? Now tell it to me."*

This simple statement shows an awesome understanding of God.

• Joseph understands that God gives and interprets dreams.

• He also knows that he, as God's servant, has a direct connection to God and thus the supernatural eyesight to see the interpretation of their dreams for them.

The baker and the cup bearer tell Joseph their dreams and he interprets them. To the cup bearer, Joseph interprets the dream as good; he will be restored. To the baker, Joseph interprets the dream as bad; he will be hanged.

The interpretations come true, of course, demonstrating that Joseph has incredible insight into the spiritual realm.

But this smaller test of his ability to hear specifically from God will soon be tested by an exponentially more significant person — the Pharaoh himself, ruler of the most powerful nation in the world.

Two years later, Joseph is still in the prison, and Pharaoh has his famous dream:

"Seven cows were going up from the river, beautiful of appearance and fat of flesh; and they were eating in the reeds. And, behold, seven other cows were going up after them from the river, evil of appearance and lean of flesh. And they were standing beside the cows on the bank of the river. And the evil-appearing and lean-fleshed cows were eating the seven cows of beautiful and fat appearance."   *Genesis 41:2-4*

Pharaoh then wakes up and falls asleep again, dreaming a second dream:

"Seven ears of grain were coming up on one stalk, fat and good. And, behold, seven ears of grain, lean and blasted by the east wind, sprouting forth after them. And the seven lean ears were swallowing the seven fat and full ears."   *Genesis 41:5-7*

Pharaoh calls for his magicians and "wise men." But none of them are able to interpret the dream for him. This doesn't mean that nobody *tried* to interpret the dream. What it means is that nobody was able to come up with a *satisfactory* interpretation for Pharaoh.

The cup-bearer remembers Joseph from two years ago, and recommends him to Pharaoh.

Pharaoh tells Joseph he has heard of him and that he's
heard Joseph is an interpreter of dreams.

Joseph, who clearly understands God's principles, is
quick to, based upon his supernatural understanding, give
the credit to God:

"Not I! God will answer the welfare of Pharaoh."
                                        Genesis 41:16

Pharaoh repeats his dream to Joseph. Joseph, drawing
on the source he gave credit to — God and his intensely
personal relationship with Him, informs Pharaoh that both
dreams contain in effect one message.

"God has shown Pharaoh what He is about to do. The
seven good cows, they are seven years; and the seven
good ears, they are seven years; it is one dream. And the
seven thin and evil-appearing cows going up after them,
they are seven years. And the seven empty ears blasted by
the east wind, they are seven years of famine. This is the
word that I spoke to Pharaoh: what God is about to do, he
has shown Pharaoh. Behold! Seven years of great plenty
are coming in all the land of Egypt. And seven years of
famine will arise after them, and the famine will consume
the land ... And as to the dream being repeated to Pharaoh
twice, that is the thing established from God, and God is
hastening to do it."

This is a demonstration of another aspect of supernatural
eyesight: the more you dig deeper into the depths of God,
the clearer your sight will be.

And the closer you get to God, the more you'll seek to
bring praise to Him, not yourself. We have seen that pattern
three times in this chapter:

- Abraham refused to be blessed by man and risk man taking credit for God's blessings

- Jacob refused to be blessed by man and risk man taking credit for God's blessings

- Joseph refused to take credit for the actions of God in his life

These three men and Noah all had a secret that is not very secret when it comes right down to it: Seeing in the supernatural must come as a result of making yourself available for God to use, and obeying when you hear Him.

CHAPTER 4

WHAT DID MOSES SEE THAT NOBODY ELSE SAW?

If there is a central non-Christ figure in the Bible, it is certainly Moses.

Moses is the lawgiver — generally credited with authoring the first five books of the Bible, the "books of Moses."

His life is revered and honored by three of the world's largest religions — Judaism, Christianity and Islam.

His ministry was so life-changing, so paradigm-defining, that he took a rag-tag band of slaves and, in 40 years, transformed them into a mighty nation and a military machine that had tremendous success because of their single-minded devotion to the God who claimed by His very name of Jehovah that He was the ONLY God in the universe.

With singular devotion and patience, he led, taught, judged and motivated millions of people to devote their lives to God. He offered to give up his own salvation if the people who followed him were to be doomed. He stood up to the king of the most powerful nation on earth and, by careful diligence and obedience to God's word, he presided over the humbling of that king, his nations and the false gods his nation worshiped.

He found his God in the wilderness — or rather God found him — and never turned aside from Him, even when he was the only person standing for God and His righteousness.

Moses, the deliverer, the lawgiver, the nation-builder, inspired generations upon generations of Jews, Christians and Muslims alike — and when the Son of the living God came to earth to fulfill His mission, He came as a "prophet like Moses."

This man who was snatched out of the river that was a god to the Egyptians and was given an Egyptian name lived a life that became a foreshadow of the life the Lord he was serving would later live.

To this man, God revealed more of Himself than He had ever revealed in the past — and more than He would reveal in the future until the advent of Jesus Christ.

Who was this man? What did he know that no one else knew? What did he see that no one else saw? What made him great?

In short, where did Moses get his supernatural eyesight?

ESTEEMING THE REPROACH OF CHRIST

Most people are familiar with the story: Moses' mother, unwilling to let her son be killed to obey the command of the Pharaoh, sent her son down the river in a boat.

What we don't often see is that Moses' mother was supernaturally clever!

The Bible says Pharaoh, who feared that the Hebrew people would become too mighty through a huge population for the Egyptians, ordered children killed:

*"And Pharaoh commanded all his people, saying, **Every son that is born, you shall cast him into the river.** And*

you shall keep alive every daughter." Exodus 1:22, (Direct translation of Masoretic text)

But the Bible tells us that Moses' mother did not want her son killed. And, using supernatural eyesight of her own, she saw a way to keep him alive:

"And a man went from the house of Levi and took a daughter of Levi. And the woman conceived and bore a son; and she saw him, that he was beautiful. And she concealed him three months. And she was not able to hide him any longer, and she took a basket for him made of papyrus, and she daubed it with bitumen and with pitch. And she put the child in it, and placed it in the reeds by the lip of the Nile." Exodus 2:1-3

Now, Pharaoh's order had been to cast every son into the river — *AND THAT'S EXACTLY WHAT SHE DID!*

His order did not say not to cast the son into the river without a boat to keep him afloat.

We know from later scriptures that Moses' mother was a woman who served God. Now we see from this passage that she had supernatural eyesight of her own. She saw, by the Spirit of God, that she could obey the Pharaoh's order and still spare the life of her son.

And her supernatural eyesight came with an additional bonus:

"And the daughter of Pharaoh went down to bathe in the Nile. And her maidens were walking on the side of the Nile. And she saw the basket in the midst of the reeds, and sent her slavegirl and took it. And she opened it and saw the child, and, behold, a boy crying! And she had pity on him and said, This one is of the children of the Hebrews.

77

And his sister said to Pharaoh's daughter, Shall I go and call a woman for you, a nurse of the Hebrew women, that she may nurse the child for you? And Pharaoh's daughter said to her, Go. And the girl went and called the child's mother. And Pharaoh's daughter said to her, **Take this child away and nurse him for me, and I will give your wages.** *And the woman took the child and nursed him."*

Exodus 2:5-9

Moses' mother had obviously instructed her daughter to make sure the child lived. When Pharaoh's daughter had found the boy, before she had even indicated that she might keep the child, the daughter suggested that she could find a Hebrew to nurse the child *"for you"* (hint, hint).

Even more incredible, though, is that Moses' mother was not only able to secure her son's life, she was able to keep him until he was weaned — and she even got paid to do it.

That's supernatural eyesight in action!

She, by the power of the living God, was able to keep her son alive, keep him long enough to teach him about the ways of God (children were weaned much later than they are today), and she got paid to raise the son whose life she had miraculously saved!

As we see the God-empowered cleverness in his mother, we begin to see the legacy Moses inherited — and part of the reason the Bible says in Hebrews:

"By faith Moses, when he was come to years, refused to be called the son of Pharaoh's daughter; Choosing rather to suffer affliction with the people of God, than to enjoy the pleasures of sin for a season; **Esteeming the reproach**

*of **Christ** greater riches than the treasures in Egypt: for he
had respect unto the recompence of the reward."*

Hebrews 11:24-26

Has it ever struck you that the Bible says Moses, who
lived at least 1,500 years before Jesus, esteemed the
reproach of CHRIST greater than the riches of Egypt?

This verse does not say Moses esteemed the reproach of
GOD; it says he esteemed the reproach of CHRIST.

In other words, when Moses grew up, he refused to live
as an Egyptian — he knew he would have to answer to
Christ, who was a greater king than Pharaoh.

How did this man know of Christ?

He had — even then — supernatural eyesight. Though
he would develop much stronger supernatural eyesight
after his experience in the wilderness, even as a young
man, he knew a Messiah was coming, and that Messiah
wanted him.

Whether he learned these truths from his mother or
knew them through supernatural influence of the Holy
Spirit on his life, the Bible does not tell us — it simply
tells us that he knew.

Even during his days in Egypt, the Bible shows us that
the man who would become the lawgiver was consumed
with the concept of justice.

When he saw an Egyptian man abusing a Hebrew, he
intervened, slaying the Egyptian in the process. When he
later saw two Hebrews fighting, the Bible says he
approached *"the guilty one"* (Exodus 2:13) and broke up
the fight.

Even as a young man, Moses was a man of justice.

But, being driven out into the wilderness because of the killing of the Egyptian, he would soon develop supernatural eyesight on a level he could never have imagined — and a level few others in history would ever approach.

In the wilderness of Midian, Moses met and married a woman there and began to work for his father-in-law, the priest of Midian.

*As he was tending flocks for his father-in-law, "the Angel of Jehovah appeared to him in a flame of fire from the middle of a thorn bush. And he looked, and behold, the thorn bush was burning with fire, and the thorn bush was not burned up! And Moses said, I will turn aside now and see this great sight, why the thorn bush is not burned up... And God called to him from the midst of the thorn bush, and said, Moses! Moses! And he said, I am here. And He said, Do not come near here, pull off your sandals from your feet, for the place on which you are standing is holy ground. And He said, I am the God of your fathers, the God of Abraham, the God of Isaac, and the God of Jacob. **And Moses hid his face, for he feared to look upon God.**"* Exodus 3:1-6

Remember that; it is important later on in this chapter. Moses, who becomes the most tremendous prophet of all time until the advent of John the Baptist, at first feared to look upon God.

Later, as we shall see, his desire had made a complete, 180-degree turnaround, and he couldn't get enough of seeing God.

Keep this in mind, because it's one of the keys to supernatural eyesight. It's like the Psalmist later says: *"As the hart panteth after the water brooks, so panteth my soul after thee, O God. My soul thirsteth for God, for the living God: when shall I come and appear before God?"*

Psalm 42:1-2

The more you look into the depths of God, the more thirsty for Him, the hungrier for Him you become.

And Moses started from the place most of us start from — he was curious about the burning bush and he turned aside to look at it. But when he understood that he was talking to the living God, he was too timid to push in very far.

Have you been to that place?

Have you ever been in a prayer service, a church meeting or just in your prayer closet, where the presence of God was so strong that you simply feared to press in any farther?

But as you grow in Him, your desire becomes to move ever closer inside — ever deeper!

Through the burning bush, God instructs Moses that he is to go to Egypt and demand that Pharaoh let the people of God go.

On the way, something interesting and often overlooked happens.

"And it happened, on the way, in the lodging place, Jehovah met him and sought to kill him. And Zipporah took a stone and cut off her son's foreskin, and caused it to touch his feet. And she said, You are a bridegroom of blood to me. And He pulled back from him. Then she said, A bridegroom of blood, for the circumcision."

Exodus 4:24-26

81

Those who are called by God are also called to obedience.

Moses, being a Hebrew descendant of Abraham, was under the covenant God had made with Abraham that all his descendants would be circumcised. Though the Bible doesn't tell us when it happened, apparently at some point Moses and Zipporah had disagreed about their son's circumcision, and Moses had let his wife's argument prevail.

Now, though, on the way to meeting with Pharaoh, God shows Moses how serious He is about the calling on Moses' life — how can he with good conscience command Pharaoh to obey God when he himself has not obeyed in the covenant of circumcision with his son?

One of the fundamental truths of supernatural eyesight is that those who go into God's presence and see the truths He reveals through His Spirit are responsible to obey Him when He has spoken.

Moses, who was called to a deeper, more profound revelation than anyone before him, is also called to absolute obedience. God simply would not let him go to Egypt to demand that Pharaoh obey Him unless He could be sure Moses would first obey Him.

Obedience was the entire theme of the lives of the patriarchs and Moses.

As you'll see later in the chapter on the prophets, prophesying requires a tremendous amount of trust in God and an unwavering dose of supernatural eyesight. Every time the prophet prophesies, he's not only putting himself on the line with those to whom he's prophesying, he's putting himself on the line with God.

He has to be sure what he's saying is what God wants him to say — and for that, supernatural eyesight is a necessity.

So when Moses went to Pharaoh, he could not afford to make a mistake — he had to be sure that everything proceeding from his mouth was something that God had intended to proceed from his mouth.

That required an intimacy with God never before seen in Bible history — it required Moses being in complete fellowship with the God he was representing to Pharaoh.

To that end, God revealed more of Himself to Moses than He had revealed to anyone previously.

God also reveals the specific role of a prophet through an analogy:

"And Jehovah said to Moses, Come, see, I have made you a god to Pharaoh; and your brother Aaron shall be your prophet. You shall speak all that I command you, and your brother Aaron shall speak to Pharaoh." Exodus 7:1

In this analogy, Aaron is the prophet of the "god," Moses. Moses speaks to Aaron, and Aaron communicates the message to Moses' intended audience, in this case, Pharaoh.

The prophet, then, is simply one who communicates the message of God to God's intended audience. Before, we had heard of prophets and understood that their mission was as emissaries of God, but in Exodus, God reveals to Moses the prophet's specific role — hearing from God and repeating it to those God wants to hear it.

This revelation comes to us through the Bible because God revealed it to Moses, who was able to understand it in the spirit. His relationship with God had grown by leaps and bounds.

But even more, God has revealed more of Himself to Moses than He had ever revealed to anyone else. Remember, when we have supernatural eyesight, we press into God, wanting to know more, wanting to dig deeper and closer to Him.

God tells Moses:

"Now you will see what I will do to Pharaoh. For he will send them away with a strong hand; yea, he will drive them out from his land with a strong hand. And God spoke to Moses and said to him, I am Jehovah. And I appeared to Abraham, to Isaac and to Jacob as God Almighty, and by my name JEHOVAH I never made Myself known to them."
Exodus 6:1-3

In this passage, God says he was known to the patriarchs as El Sha-dda-i (אֵל שַׁדָּי), which means God Almighty, or the Almighty God. By this designation, to the unbelievers God could technically simply have been the most powerful of the gods. When He says that He was not known by his name, JEHOVAH, He's not saying that they didn't know His name (they did); He's saying that His nature as the self-existent One — the ONLY God — was not the basis of their understanding of Him.

Remember, when Jacob left the home of Laban, his wife, Rachel stole one of the household idols of Laban. Jacob, who himself worshiped no other God than Jehovah, was not upset that someone in his camp had a household idol, but only that someone had stolen one.

Though the patriarchs were monotheistic in practice, they did not condemn the polytheistic practices of the nations around them. When Pharaoh claimed to know of no god named Jehovah, Moses and Aaron answered him that Jehovah is the God of the Hebrews. But God is explaining to Moses here that He is not only the God of the Hebrews — He is Jehovah (יְהֹוָה), *the God of all.*

This is really the first post-flood declaration of monotheism in a doctrinal way. God had claimed exclusivity and supremacy before, but in this passage, He makes it crystal clear: He is the ONLY God. Period.

He revealed Himself to Abraham as the God of promise. To his sons, He revealed Himself as the God of their fathers. To Moses, however, God goes deeper, further than He has ever gone before, and He reveals Himself as the ONLY God.

It later became important, because the first of God's judgments on the Egyptians — the turning of the Nile into blood — was a judgment on one of their chief deity figures, which was the Nile itself.

The Egyptians regarded the Nile as sacred, the giver of life. After all, without it, they would have no harvest, no crops, no food, no life.

But when God judges the Nile and overwhelms it with His power, He makes an object lesson of the thing He's already told Moses: the Nile is not a god; I AM the only God.

Also, as God delivers judgments in the form of plagues on the Egyptians and their royalty, the sentiment of the Pharaoh and his people is clearly against Moses. Wouldn't it, after all, be easier to kill this shepherd and get this whole thing over with?

But Moses did not fear Pharaoh or his armies because he had received supernatural eyesight — he had seen into the spirit. He had understood that not only was the Nile not a god, but also that if God was for him, Pharaoh could threaten all he wanted but be powerless to do anything about it.

As the plagues swept over Egypt, Pharaoh increased the burdens and hardships on the people of Israel, who grumbled and complained that Moses was only hurting them.

With both Pharaoh *and Israel* against him, the pressure on Moses to pack up and slink away back into the relative safety of Midian must have been immense.

But he remembered the lesson he had learned on the way at the place of lodging — God required obedience above all other things. With that knowledge and the knowledge that God is the only God, Moses was able to persevere when everyone wanted him to stop — and he was able to prevail by the power of God over the mightiest nation on the planet.

But the lessons and the deepening of Moses' relationship with God was only beginning.

As he led the children of Israel through the wilderness, God determined that He would see if the children of Israel would behave like Abraham, Isaac, Jacob and Joseph had. The patriarchs had obeyed God and lived their lives according to His direction simply because He had asked them to.

The covenant God had with them was simple: Listen and obey Me, and I'll bless you and make you a great nation.

Read that paragraph again, because it's fundamentally important to understanding what you're about to read.

God required no fancy rituals of them.

He required no funny clothes.

He required no set, specific religious prayers.

When the children of Israel in the wilderness were grumbling about the lack of food, God determined that He would test them.

What they were grumbling about was not the complete lack of food; they were griping about the *lack of variety.* After all, they had flocks and animals with them. They had meal, flour and other necessities.

They wanted the same luxuries they had in Egypt. Though they were slaves, Egypt was a stable economy with a predictable cycle of flooding, harvesting and eating.

Out in the wilderness, they had to depend on God, and the children of Israel did not like it.

First, they complained about the lack of water, and God performed a miracle to give them water. Then he gave them their first promises, and their first warning:

*"He made a statute and an ordinance for them there, and He tested them there. And He said, If you carefully listen to the voice of Jehovah your God, and you do what is right in His eyes, **and you give ear to His commandments,** and keep all His statutes, I will not put on you all the diseases which I have put on Egypt; for I am Jehovah your healer."*
Exodus 15:25-26

This covenant is similar to the one Abraham had; listen and obey and the blessings will come.

But the children of Israel, though they agreed with their mouths, did not agree with their hearts. They later begin grumbling about lack of food.

*"And Jehovah said to Moses, Behold, I AM! Bread will rain from the heavens for you. And the people shall go out and gather the matter of a day in its day, **so that I may test them, whether they will walk in My law or not.** And it shall be on the sixth day they shall prepare what they bring in. And it shall be double what they gather day by day."*   *Exodus 16:4-5*

It's interesting here that God equates "law" with "instructions."

The word translated "law" is "torah" (תּוֹרָה), which is what the Jews call the Bible.

But the word regarding gathering of manna is not officially part of the Law as we know it. Indeed, the Law had not yet been delivered. What God is saying here is that He will prove the Israelites to demonstrate whether they'll obey Him or not. Remember, the secret to supernatural eyesight — and the secret to a relationship with God is listening to Him and obeying what you hear.

The Torah that we have today is simply the written-down word of God. But to God, the "Torah" is His word — His instructions to us.

If we obey those instructions, we are His servants. If we don't, we are not. Today, Christians have the "Torah" written on their hearts — the instructions of God come directly from the Holy Spirit into our hearts.

Moses, using his supernatural eyesight to discern exactly what's going on, lets the people know exactly whom they're complaining against:

"Your murmurings are not against us, but against Jehovah."
Exodus 16:8

He understands that the people believe it is Moses who has led them out of Egypt, and they don't understand it is God who had done it.

In grumbling, they think they're expressing dissatisfaction with Moses' leadership, but in reality, they're expressing displeasure with God.

This is a demonstration of the difference between those who see in the supernatural and those who don't! Those who see in the spirit understand the spiritual truth. Those who don't look for a physical answer to everything they see. Though they had experienced tremendous miracles in God's deliverance, they still blamed a man, Moses, for the predicament in which they found themselves.

Their disobedience is why God delivers the Law to them.

There is a tremendous difference between the relationship God has with Moses and the one He has with the children of Israel.

As Moses goes up to the mountain to speak with God and receive the law for the Israelites, he approaches the presence of God directly, without ritual, without preparation.

When he talks to God, it is almost informal.

Remembering back to the story of Abraham, we can see a parallel. Abraham was sitting at the door of his tent when God simply arrived and began talking to him.

There was no ritual, no special clothing — nothing. It was simply a conversation between God and man.

When Moses talked to God, there also was no ritual, no preparation. It was simply God speaking to a man He considered His friend.

But when God delivered the Law for the worship of Israel, there were tremendous rituals that had to be kept:

"And you shall take to yourself your brother Aaron, and his sons with him, from among the sons of Israel, for him to serve as priest to Me; Aaron, Nadab, and Abihu, Eleazar, and Ithamar, the sons of Aaron. And you shall make holy garments for your brother Aaron, for glory and for beauty And you shall speak to all the wise-hearted whom I have filled with a spirit of wisdom; and they shall make the garments of Aaron to sanctify him for his serving as priest to Me." Exodus 28:1-3

This is interesting, because God says it is the garments of Aaron (and presumably all the priests) that will sanctify him to God.

The word "sanctify" here is qadash, which means to be set apart; consecrated.

Moses, however, was apparently set apart and consecrated without all the get-up. He needed no tunic, no breastplate, no Urim and Thummim, no laver, no tabernacle, no ritual washing to enter into the presence of God and be consecrated to God.

The one who delivered the ordinances was EXEMPT from the ordinances he delivered.

In Exodus 29, God says this after He has described all the sacrifices He'll be requiring from the people:

"And I will meet the sons of Israel there (at the door of the tabernacle) and it shall be sanctified by my glory. And I will sanctify the tabernacle of the congregation and the altar. And I will sanctify Aaron and his sons to minister as priests to Me. And I will dwell in the midst of the sons of Israel; and I will be God to them."

Verses 43-45

When Abram was 99 years old, God said, *"Walk before me and be perfect, and I will make My covenant between Me and you..."* Genesis 17:1-2

Abraham's promise from God was simple; there was no complicated religion to keep, no complicated garments, no complicated tabernacle.

God did not need an ark to meet Abraham, He met him at the door of Abraham's own tent.(Genesis 18:1)

To the children of Israel, however, God required that they build a tent especially for meeting, make elaborate sacrifices and perform elaborate rituals.

Only AFTER that would God meet them at the door of the tent they had prepared especially for that purpose:

"This shall be a continual burnt offering to your generations, at the door of the tabernacle of the congregation before the face of Jehovah; there where I meet with you to speak to you there." Exodus 29:42

The parallel is fascinating.

Abraham was simply obeying God because of the covenant he had made with Him in Genesis 17.

But in Genesis 18, God showed up to the door of Abram's tent without any special preparation.

However, because of the nature of the covenant God made with the Israelites, His meeting with them was more formal, and required vast preparation on their parts.

The difference in their relationship with God is obvious, and indicative of the nature of the people making the covenant.

God had not changed.

But unlike Abraham, the children of Israel were not of a mind to serve God — they agreed to keep His covenant when His presence was obvious, but after He had apparently left them alone for a while, they always reverted to their own ways.

This difference was the reason they needed a law, and the reason their covenant was so much more elaborate than Abraham's.

In Exodus 30:11-12, it becomes clear that the Israelites' relationship with God has changed significantly from what Abraham's relationship was:

"And Jehovah spoke to Moses, saying: When you lift up the head of the sons of Israel, of those numbered, each one shall give the ransom of his soul to Jehovah when numbering them; and there shall not be a plague among them when numbering them."

The word "ransom" in this passage is "rpeko", which means the price of a life.

With Abraham, the sacrifice was a sacrifice of thanksgiving — largely an expression of worship. With the Israelites, it is a sin offering, a ransom for their very lives, which they had forfeited by breaking the covenant.

The fundamental nature of the relationship between God and His people had changed. These were people who did not by nature serve God, but because they had made a covenant, they were required to serve Him or die.

The nature of their covenant was obligatory — they made a formal pledge to obey God and serve Him only.

The covenant of Abraham was different in that, while the obedience and exclusivity were understood, they were not explicitly stated.

In other words, that Abraham would serve no other gods was a foregone conclusion; there was no possibility that he would go astray, so it was not included in the covenant.

With Israel, however, the possibility was real that they would go astray and serve other gods, so the exclusivity was written into the covenant, and when broken, became a death sentence on those who broke it.

Thus, while Abraham gave sacrifices of thanksgiving to God, Israel had to give sacrifices of ransom to God.

Even the ritual washing, which is codified in Exodus 30:17-21, signifies that even the priests are dirty, and the ceremony of washing themselves is symbolic of the cleansing they must go through to enter the presence of God:

"And Jehovah spoke to Moses, saying: And you shall make a laver of bronze, and its base bronze, for washing. And you shall put it between the tabernacle of the

*congregation and the altar; and you shall put water there.
And Aaron and his sons shall wash from it, their hands
and their feet, as they go into the tabernacle of the
congregation they shall wash with water, and shall not
die; or as they draw near to the altar to minister, to burn
a fire offering to Jehovah. And they shall wash their
hands and their feet, and shall not die. And it shall be a
never-ending statute to them, to him and to his seed for
their generations."*

But Moses, as I said earlier, who delivered this Law, did
not have to go through all these rituals to enter the
presence of God.

The reason was that Moses, as Abraham before him, was
a man whose heart was committed to obeying God and
worshiping Him alone.

He would never dream of making a graven image, or
of praying to another god. He would never dream of
breaking the word God had given him, so God felt no
need to write down a list of rules for Moses, because
Moses had pressed inward to God and had
supernatural eyesight.

Paul later explained it like this:

*"Knowing this, **that the law is not made for a righteous
man, but for the lawless and disobedient**, for the ungodly
and for sinners, for unholy and profane, for murderers of
fathers and murderers of mothers, for manslayers."*
1 Timothy 1:9

The law was given for those who, by nature, did not
desire to serve God. Those who worshiped Him —
Abraham, Isaac, Jacob, Joseph and Moses — had no need
for a law; they were His servants already.

In this, God reveals to Moses an even deeper portion of His own nature than before. Moses has seen into the spirit and has seen that God is *"a rewarder of them that diligently seek him."*   Hebrews 11:6

THE SHADOW OF THINGS TO COME

But Moses spiritual insight and eyesight was deeper than things many have ever considered. Not only was he able to see and understand the nature of God better than any man before him, he was able to see things that no man after him — with the exception of Jesus — would see and understand.

The writer of Hebrews makes an interesting statement in the New Testament about Moses:

*"For every high priest is ordained to offer gifts and sacrifices: wherefore it is of necessity that this man have somewhat also to offer. For if he were on earth, he should not be a priest, seeing that there are priests that offer gifts according to the law: Who serve unto the example and shadow of heavenly things, **as Moses was admonished of God when he was about to make the tabernacle: for, See, saith he, that thou make all things according to the pattern shewed to thee in the mount."***
Hebrews 8:3-5

The writer of Hebrews continues: *"For the law **having a shadow of good things to come, and not the very image of the things,** can never with those sacrifices which they offered year by year continually make the comers thereunto perfect."*   Hebrews 10:1

Paul had earlier spoken of this same thing, saying: *"For now we see through a glass, darkly; but then face to face:*

*now I know in part; but then shall I know even as also I
am known."*   *1 Corinthians 13:12*

The New Testament writers are attempting to convey
that the patterns Moses revealed of the thing saw in the
mountain were *but a shadow* of the heavenly things
they represent.

The tabernacle was a shadow of the heavenly tabernacle...

The Ark of the Covenant was a shadow of God's throne
in heaven...

The priests' garments were a shadow of the clothing the
angels who minister before God day and night wear...

The ritual washing the priests had to endure was but a
SHADOW of the washing in the blood that was to come
through Jesus!

But the point in this book is that MOSES SAW
THOSE THINGS THAT WERE BUT A SHADOW IN
THE PATTERNS HE BROUGHT DOWN FROM
THE MOUNTAIN!

With his supernatural eyesight, Moses was able to peer
into the very heaven itself and see the things that he later
represented with the earthly things.

The tabernacle could never actually show the glory that
is heaven — Moses could only represent it in a shadow
with earthly things.

The Ark of the Covenant could never actually match the
glory of God's throne — Moses had to represent it with
the most precious thing on earth, gold.

Never before had a prophet — or any man, for that matter — seen into heaven and beheld the awesome things that were contained therein. Even Moses could not completely digest it all without consequence; his face glowed by that and the thing he saw next, which to this day boggles the mind.

UNMATCHED INTIMACY WITH GOD

Chapter 33 of Exodus begins with God instructing Moses:

"And Jehovah spoke to Moses, Come, go up from here, you and the people whom you have caused to go up out from the land of Egypt, to the land that I swore to Abraham, to Isaac and to Jacob, saying, I will give it to your seed. And I will send an angel before your face, and I will drive out the Canaanites, the Amorites and the Hittites, and the Perizzites, the Hivites and the Jebusites; to a land flowing with milk and honey. For I will not go up among you, for you are a stiff-necked people, lest I consume you in the way."   *Exodus 33:1-3*

God says He will fulfill His word and give the land to the Israelites, but He won't go with them, because they are stubborn, and if His presence is with them, He might have to consume them in the way.

This is bad news. If God won't go with them, they're doomed, even if He initially drives their enemies out from before them.

The people mourn when they hear the bad news, but God explains that He would consume them in an instant if He came up in the midst of them:

"And the people heard this evil word, and they mourned, and did not put any ornaments on himself. And

97

Jehovah said to Moses, Say to the sons of Israel, You are a stiff-necked people; in one instant I will go up among you and I will consume you. And now lay off from you your ornaments, that I may know what I shall do to you. And the sons of Israel pulled off their ornaments, from Mount Horeb."   *Exodus 33:4-6*

Moses, however, continues his now-all-consuming quest to know more of God, to get deeper into His presence:

"And Moses took the tent and pitched it outside the camp, far off from the camp. And he called it the tabernacle of the congregation. And it happened that everyone seeking Jehovah went to the tabernacle of the congregation that was outside the camp. And it happened as Moses went to the tabernacle, the people all rose and stood, each one at the door of his tent. And they looked after Moses until he had gone into the tabernacle. And it happened as Moses went into the tabernacle, the pillar of cloud would come down and stand at the door of the tabernacle. And He spoke with Moses."
                                     Exodus 33:7-9

As the man of God comes into the tent to speak with Him, God demonstrates to all who see that He is with Moses and that Moses has achieved a relationship with Him that few others have achieved. Even in the days of the patriarchs, God did not visit His people this often or in such a miraculous way.

But the most awesome thing is this:

"And Jehovah would speak to Moses face to face, as a man speaks with his friend."   *Exodus 33:11*

This is important, because it establishes the level of relationship Moses had with God. Where the priests would be required to go through an incredible amount of ritual cleansing and whatnot, Moses could simply enter the tabernacle and, as Abraham before him, communicate with God as old friends.

It's a stark contrast to the religion that Moses later hands down, and it bears mentioning that the contrast is there for our instruction. The religion was handed down to "a stiff-necked people," whom God had wanted to destroy not once, but many different times. God was willing to fulfill His promise to Abraham by giving the people the land, but He was not willing to be in the midst of the people to whom He was giving the promise — He wasn't their friend, because they rejected Him.

So Moses had to move the tent *outside the camp,* where God would meet with him face-to-face.

The difference between Moses and the people he led was that Moses was a *friend* of God; the people were not.

That friendship is Moses' key to supernatural eyesight — it is the foundation for everything he did for God for the rest of his life.

It was why he could meet God face-to-face without any special ritual; the people could not.

The chapter continues with Moses speaking to God:

"And Moses said to Jehovah, Behold, You are saying to me, cause this people to go up. And You, You have not told me whom You will send with me. And yet you have said, I know you by name, and also you have found favor in My eyes. And now, if I have found favor in Your eyes, please make me see Your ways, and let me know You, so

that I may find favor in Your eyes; and consider that this nation is Your people."   Exodus 33:12-13

Moses is pleading with God: You say I'm Your friend, but You haven't let me in on what You're planning to do. You've told me to lead Israel, but You won't tell me anything more.

He wants God to let him know God — to understand Him.

God answers Moses:

"And He said, My presence will go with you, and I will give you rest."   Exodus 33:14

In other words, set your mind at ease. I'll go with you. I'll take care of you. You want to know whom I'm sending with you — I'm coming along Myself.

Moses is relieved, but he reiterates his dependence on God: *"If Your presence does not go, do not cause us to go up from here."*   Verse 15

Now, if we think about it, this verse may seem anathema to modern thinking. Moses is, in effect, saying, "I don't want an angel to go with us as you said earlier. If You don't come with us, please don't make us go at all."

But Moses is simply doing the same thing Abraham earlier did and Jesus later did: He is being honest with God! Our modern sensibilities don't like to think of speaking our minds with God. But Moses spoke his mind: he did not want God's messenger — he wanted God Himself.

Most of us today would be thrilled and turn a few loops if God promised that His angels would accompany us on a journey. But Moses wanted God Himself, and he wasn't afraid to let God know what was on his heart. That's what friends do — they're honest with each other.

He goes further:

"And now by what can it be known that I and Your people have found favor in Your eyes? Is it not in Your going with us? And we are distinguished, I and Your people, from all the nations which are on the face of the earth?"

Exodus 33:16

He says, basically, that an angel may go with any old nation, and God's will can be accomplished through any nation by way of an angel.

But Israel will be distinguished because God Himself is going before them — it is a sign to all that the nation has found favor in God's eyes.

This understanding of Moses came because God has revealed it to him — his friendship with God, his loving relationship with God has made him perceptive. He has supernatural eyesight.

In any case, after God tells Moses that He will accompany them, Moses continues, getting to the most amazing moment in the Old Testament:

"And he said, I pray, let me see Your glory. And He said, I will cause all My goodness to pass before your face. And I will call out the name of Jehovah before your face. And I will favor whom I will favor, and I will have mercy on whom I will have mercy. And he said, You are not able to see My face; for no man sees Me and lives."

Verses 18-20

This is interesting because earlier in this same chapter, the Bible says Moses spoke with God face-to-face.

Clearly, speaking to Moses face-to-face is different than Moses actually seeing God's face. Seeing God is possibly not the same as a deeper level of seeing Him. Moses, after all, talked with God casually — as a friend talks to a friend. But he still wanted to see God's glory.

The word "glory" there is "dbokf", which means weight, but only figuratively in a good sense, such as splendor or *copiousness*.

Moses was requesting a deeper intimacy with God.

This man who spoke to God face-to-face, who spoke to Him as a friend would speak to a friend, DID NOT HAVE ENOUGH OF GOD IN HIS LIFE YET! *HE WANTED MORE!*

He wanted to see God's copiousness — His weightiness. He wanted to see the fullness of God.

This lends itself to the idea that there is one kind of "seeing God," such as Abraham standing by the door of his tent conversing with God, and a deeper kind of seeing God — in His fullness — that Moses was able to do except for God's face.

And God, who considers Moses His friend, is willing for Moses to see all of Him up to the part that would kill Moses. No man before, and no man until Jesus would see more of God. Moses got closer to God than any purely mortal man in history — because no matter how much he got of God, he ALWAYS WANTED MORE.

"And Jehovah said, Behold, a place by Me! And you shall stand on a rock. And as My glory is passing it will be that I will put you in a cleft of the rock; and I will cover My palm over you during my passing. And I will remove My palm, and you shall see My back; but My face cannot be seen."   *Verses 21-22*

Moses' relationship with God continues to be a deepening contrast with the Israelites. Their only desire is to serve themselves. Moses' only desire is to know God more deeply. Thus, when the two are to come in the presence of God, the manner in which they are to do it highlights the contrast. Moses can simply enter the presence of God as a friend would approach a friend. The Israelites must send a priest, who must perform all kinds of rituals — like a stranger.

That is the key to the supernatural eyesight Moses received. It's the key to why this man who was pulled out of the river by the daughter of a pagan king became the central figure in the Old Testament.

It's the key to why he, as no man before him, was able to understand the deep things of God.

It's the key to why his successor, Joshua, was able to carry on the incredible role Moses had framed for him.

JOSHUA'S UNDERSTANDING OF THE COVENANT

Joshua was with Moses on the mountain. When Moses talked to God in the tabernacle, Joshua was there in the tabernacle — in fact, he made a practice of never leaving the tabernacle during that time.

Joshua, in fact, was such a servant to Moses that his name later became the name of our Lord.

"Jesus" is the Greek version of the Hebrew word "יְהוֹשֻׁעַ;", which means Jehovah saved, and is pronounced in English as "Joshua."

Joshua had a deep understanding — a deep supernatural eyesight — that almost certainly got its foundation from his proximity to Moses. His desires closely reflected those of Moses; he wanted to know God intimately as Moses had.

In the book of Joshua, the great leader gives a final appeal to the Israelites:

"And now fear Jehovah and serve Him in sincerity and truth, and turn away from the gods that your fathers served beyond the river, and in Egypt; and you serve Jehovah."   *Joshua 24:14*

You notice right off the bat that he mentions the fact that, even after God had delivered the children of Israel from Egypt, they served false gods in the desert.

But now he's admonishing them to serve God — and forsake all the false gods they had served before.

"And if it seems evil in your eyes to serve Jehovah, choose for you today whom you will serve — whether the gods whom your fathers served beyond the river, or the gods of the Amorites in whose land you are living — but as for me and my house, we will serve Jehovah."
Verse 15

Now, many times the Church takes this as a great anthem, but they stop right there and ignore the greater context in which it was written and spoken.

Everyone loves to say it: "as for me and my house, we will serve the Lord."

How righteous it sounds.

How committed.

It sounds downright holy.

But Joshua is making a clear statement here that many overlook — he's saying listen, you've got to decide right now whom you'll serve. If you're not going to serve God, just go ahead right now and say you're going to serve the false gods of your fathers or the false gods of the Amorites.

Do whatever you want, but today *make a choice.*

The people do the predictable thing — they do the thing they think Joshua and God want them to do. Remember, God does not want lip service; He doesn't want us to say what we think He wants us to say. He wants us to say *what's in our hearts.* But the people of Israel have not taken the mask off:

"And the people replied and said, Far be it from us to forsake Jehovah, to serve other gods. For Jehovah our God is He who has brought us and our fathers out of the land of Egypt...We also will serve Jehovah, for He is our God." Joshua 24:16-18

It sounds good, doesn't it?

What more could Joshua ask for? He told them to make a choice, and they've now told him that they had indeed made their choice — they'll serve God, thank you very much.

You would think he would be happy, they'd throw a party and that would be the end of the chapter.

But it's not.

*"And Joshua said to the people, **You cannot serve Jehovah,** for He is a holy God; He is a jealous God. He will not lift up from you your transgressions or your sins. When you forsake Jehovah and shall serve strange gods, then He will turn away and do evil to you, and consume you, after He has done good to you."*   *Verses 19-20*

They told Joshua what they thought he wanted to hear, but he didn't want to hear them lie — he wanted the truth.

Joshua calls them a bunch of liars.

He essentially said, "you're lying to me. You won't serve God — you CAN'T serve God. And if you now say you will, when you turn away and worship the false gods, you'll just have been postponing the inevitable; God will judge you and it won't be pretty."

Now, just after you've said something like, I'll serve God, the last thing you want to hear is, "Sorry, no. You can't do it. Go home."

And the people insist that they're not lying; "Oh, no, Joshua, we're serious. We'll serve Him."

"And the people said to Joshua, No but we will serve Jehovah."   *Verse 21*

This is where they get themselves into trouble. It would have been easier for them if they had just told the truth right here.

They say with their mouth that they'll serve Him — but they've written a check with their mouths that they can't back up with their actions! They don't have the money to pay when it comes time for the check to go through the bank!

*"And Joshua said to the people, **You are witnesses against yourselves**, that you have chosen Jehovah for yourselves, to serve Him."* Verse 22

This is what they didn't understand — and what Joshua understood because he had supernatural eyesight. They became witnesses against themselves. They testified that they indeed had made a covenant to worship God. And when they broke that covenant, there was no need for a trial; they themselves were the witnesses for the prosecution!

They had said, "Yes, Lord," but they didn't have the gumption to keep their own word!

Jesus reiterated Joshua's admonition as he told this parable:

*"If any man come to me, and hate not his father, and mother, and wife, and children, and brethren, and sisters, yea, and his own life also, he cannot be my disciple. And whosoever doth not bear his cross, and come after me, cannot be my disciple. **For which of you, intending to build a tower, sitteth not down first, and counteth the cost, whether he have sufficient to finish it? Lest haply, after he hath laid the foundation, and is not able to finish it, all that behold it begin to mock him, Saying, This man began to build, and was not able to finish. Or what king, going to make war against another king, sitteth not down first, and consulteth whether he be able with ten thousand to meet him that cometh against him with twenty thousand? Or else, while the other is yet a***

great way off, he sendeth an ambassage, and desireth conditions of peace. So likewise, whosoever he be of you that forsaketh not all that he hath, he cannot be my disciple. Salt is good: but if the salt have lost his savour, wherewith shall it be seasoned? It is neither fit for the land, nor yet for the dunghill; but men cast it out. He that hath ears to hear, let him hear."   Luke 14:26-35

It would have been better if the man had never tried to build the tower at all.

He would not have wasted his money or his time. He would have not been out anything.

And Jesus finished His admonition like this: *"This people draweth nigh unto me with their mouth, and honoureth me with their lips; but their heart is far from me."*

Matthew 15:8

Hundreds of years before Jesus came to the earth, Joshua had peered into the Spirit and understood the principle Jesus was using because he had supernatural eyesight. He understood the deep things of God.

Like Moses, he saw things that nobody else saw. He received revelations from God that confounded those who did not understand.

CHAPTER 5

THE PROPHETS SEE AND TRANSLATE THE SPIRITUAL INTO THE NATURAL

When I preach in nations of the world where the primary language is not English, I could not communicate to the Nationals in those countries in the language of my birth.

I was born in America. From the time I was a little boy, my primary language has been English.

I cannot communicate with people who speak Russian. I can't communicate with people who speak Mandarin Chinese.

In order to communicate with those people, I must have something that becomes a very valuable commodity on the foreign mission fields.

I must have a translator.

A translator is someone who speaks at least two languages — English and the language of the country in which I am preaching.

The recent terrorist attacks on New York City and Washington, D.C. led to a call from the federal government in the United States.

As President George W. Bush issued his call for war on terrorism and the nations that harbored terrorists, he focused his attentions on Osama bin Laden, an Arabic-speaking rogue who hid under a twisted perversion of Islam for his reasoning in terrorism.

As part of the "war on terrorism," the federal government began calling for U.S. citizens who spoke both English and Arabic as part of the intelligence-gathering efforts.

The skill is invaluable. Without translators, it would be impossible for the intelligence community to understand the language of the people they were tracking down, and therefore it would be impossible to find them and capture them.

Similarly, our war is on the devil and his angels.

Our goal is to lead souls to Christ — but we cannot communicate the message of the gospel to those who do not speak English if we don't first find a translator.

Thus, translators are invaluable in communicating a message between one side and another.

But have you ever thought about what a translator does?

The translator, who has a primary language, learns a secondary language and, comparing the words in the second language to concepts he learned in the first language, takes the second language's concepts and describes them in the first language.

In Hebrew, the word Elohim stands for God. In English, we use the word "God." But if you said the word "God" to someone who only spoke Hebrew, he wouldn't know what you were talking about. A translator takes the English word "God" and, knowing that "God" stands for the Deity who revealed Himself through the Hebrew Bible,

interprets that concept and puts it into the Hebrew word
"Elohim," which he knows means the same thing.

The reason I have spent so much time on the role
of a translator is the concept is important — all truth
is parallel.

What is true in the natural is paralleled by an equal truth
in the spirit.

In the natural, human translators interpret human languages,
deciphering one language and distilling it into another.

In the spirit, translators see the "language" of the spirit,
deciphering God's will, His nature and His commands,
and they distill it into the "language" of the natural.

You see, the natural mind cannot comprehend the spirit.

Here's what the Bible has to say about it:

" *For they that are after the flesh do mind the things of
the flesh; but they that are after the Spirit the things of the
Spirit. For to be carnally minded is death; but to be
spiritually minded is life and peace. Because the carnal
mind is enmity against God: for it is not subject to the law
of God, neither indeed can be.*" *Romans 8:5-7*

Those who are in the flesh understand flesh. Those who
are in the spirit understand spirit. The two are unable to
communicate to each other — without a translator.

God, through the ages, has required that His message be
delivered to carnal man.

In those cases, He has used translators: the prophets.

A prophet, then, is someone who can, with supernatural

eyesight, see into the spirit, hear the message of God and, translating it, distribute it into the natural.

God is Spirit. His message is Spirit.

Man is natural. His understanding is natural.

The natural man can't understand the message of the Spirit without a translator. The prophets look into the spirit realm, understand the message and speak it in ways that the man of flesh can understand.

When a human preacher uses a translator, he must be able to implicitly trust that translator. After all, if the primary speaker does not speak the language that is being translated, the translator must be trusted to accurately represent the preaching in the language into which he is translating it.

An unscrupulous translator can take a message and make it say whatever he wants it to say, and the people who are being preached to would never know the difference.

Similarly, God calls men and women to be prophets that He knows will accurately translate His desires, which are communicated in spirit, into the natural.

Thus, the prophet's life was separated, different than the lives of those around him.

He was sanctified, separated, called and set apart from his peers.

He had to be separate, because he could not let influence from people taint the message God had called him to deliver. He could not be tempted by money to change the message of God. He could not be frightened from preaching at threat of his life.

The prophet had to be dedicated completely to supernatural eyesight. He had to be completely given over to knowing God and His nature. He had to be committed to clearly understanding God's message and the way He wanted it communicated.

That understanding is made clear in the first chapter of Daniel:

"In the third year of the reign of Jehoiakim king of Judah came Nebuchadnezzar king of Babylon unto Jerusalem, and besieged it. And the Lord gave Jehoiakim king of Judah into his hand, with part of the vessels of the house of God: which he carried into the land of Shinar to the house of his god; and he brought the vessels into the treasure house of his god. And the king spake unto Ashpenaz the master of his eunuchs, that he should bring certain of the children of Israel, and of the king's seed, and of the princes; Children in whom was no blemish, but well favoured, and skilful in all wisdom, and cunning in knowledge, and understanding science, and such as had ability in them to stand in the king's palace, and whom they might teach the learning and the tongue of the Chaldeans. And the king appointed them a daily provision of the king's meat, and of the wine which he drank: so nourishing them three years, that at the end thereof they might stand before the king. Now among these were of the children of Judah, Daniel, Hananiah, Mishael, and Azariah: ... But Daniel purposed in his heart that he would not defile himself with the portion of the king's meat, nor with the wine which he drank: therefore he requested of the prince of the eunuchs that he might not defile himself. ... And the prince of the eunuchs said unto Daniel, I fear my lord the king, who hath appointed your meat and your drink: for why should he see your faces worse liking than the children which are of your sort?

*Then shall ye make me endanger my head to the king.
Then said Daniel to Melzar, whom the prince of the
eunuchs had set over Daniel, Hananiah, Mishael, and
Azariah, Prove thy servants, I beseech thee, ten days; and
let them give us pulse to eat, and water to drink. Then let
our countenances be looked upon before thee, and the
countenance of the children that eat of the portion of the
king's meat: and as thou seest, deal with thy servants. So
he consented to them in this matter, and proved them ten
days. And at the end of ten days their countenances
appeared fairer and fatter in flesh than all the children
which did eat the portion of the king's meat. Thus Melzar
took away the portion of their meat, and the wine that they
should drink; and gave them pulse."* Daniel 1:1-16

Daniel, who understood that he was called to serve God,
even if that meant falling out of favor with the king, or
even his death. He refused to eat the king's meat, because
he was sanctified to God. He understood that the prophet
must be separated — and he believed God to keep him
and the three other Hebrew children safe and undefiled.

As a result of such trust in God, God used Daniel to
prophesy some of the most stunning prophecies in the
Bible. Daniel was the first prophet in the Bible to
prophesy about the antichrist. He accurately prophesied
about the coming Persian empire, the Greek/Macedonian
empire and finally the Roman empire.

He was able to interpret the dreams of the Babylonian
king. He was able to prophesy — to the king — the last
king of Babylon's demise at the hands of the Medo-
Persians. He was able to accurately prophesy — TO THE
VERY YEAR — the advent of Jesus Christ.

All these things had their beginning in Daniel's ability to see into the spirit world with supernatural eyesight and realize that he and his friends were to stay sanctified — set apart — so they could accurately deliver God's message to the carnal people of Babylon.

Isaiah also found himself at odds with the rest of mankind as he separated himself from them.

Ezekiel found his very body being used as a sign to the people he was called to reach.

Hosea was called upon to marry a prostitute as a symbolic representation of God's relationship with Israel. As Hosea's wife was a harlot, Israel, too had strayed from God and had gone whoring after the false gods of the nations around Israel.

The prophet Samuel provides an object lesson of one of the great prophets of all time. Most of us know the story about how Hannah, Samuel's mother, was barren and prayed to God to give her a child. She promised God that if he granted her a child, she would dedicate the child to God's service. True to her word, she dedicated Samuel to the service of God, and he grew up in the house of the Lord in Shiloh, where he ministered to Eli the priest.

When Samuel was a small boy, God began calling to him to speak out against the unrighteousness of Eli ignoring the perversions of his sons.

The Lord calls to Samuel as he is asleep. Samuel does not recognize the voice of the Lord — he is, after all, a little child.

He instead assumes that Eli is the one calling him, and he goes to Eli to ask what Eli wants. Eli, of course, didn't call the boy, so he sends him back. This happens twice. But the third time, Eli understands that the voice calling Samuel is the voice of the Lord, and he instructs the boy to answer the voice and listen to what it says.

Then this happens:

"And the LORD came, and stood, and called as at other times, Samuel, Samuel. Then Samuel answered, Speak; for thy servant heareth. And the LORD said to Samuel, Behold, I will do a thing in Israel, at which both the ears of every one that heareth it shall tingle. In that day I will perform against Eli all things which I have spoken concerning his house: when I begin, I will also make an end. For I have told him that I will judge his house for ever for the iniquity which he knoweth; because his sons made themselves vile, and he restrained them not. And therefore I have sworn unto the house of Eli, that the iniquity of Eli's house shall not be purged with sacrifice nor offering for ever. And Samuel lay until the morning, and opened the doors of the house of the LORD. **And Samuel feared to shew Eli the vision.** *Then Eli called Samuel, and said, Samuel, my son. And he answered, Here am I. And he said, What is the thing that the LORD hath said unto thee?* **I pray thee hide it not from me: God do so to thee, and more also, if thou hide any thing from me of all the things that he said unto thee. And Samuel told him every whit,** *and hid nothing from him. And he said, It is the LORD: let him do what seemeth him good. And Samuel grew, and the LORD was with him, and* **did let none of his words fall to the ground."** *1 Samuel 3:10-19*

Samuel heard a message from God that was not pleasant for Eli.

The message was of doom, gloom and destruction.

Samuel was a little boy, who served Eli as both a priest and a father figure. It's quite easy to understand how he might have been reticent to tell Eli the bad news that God had given him.

But Eli tells Samuel that, if he doesn't reveal the news, the same things prophesied would happen to him.

(That, by the way, shows that Eli knew the news was bad before it was ever delivered)

Samuel, who knows God's word is true, spills his guts, and tells Eli everything. And the boy learned an important lesson — as a prophet, he was called to reveal God's word, no matter how difficult that may be.

Because of the faithfulness that Samuel showed in translating God's spiritual message into the language of the natural that Eli would understand, God gave Samuel an incredible eyesight into the supernatural. In fact, Samuel's ability to see and prophesy God's will and His doings was so incredible that NONE OF HIS WORDS EVER FAILED TO COME TRUE.

His prophecies were so unfailingly accurate that when he went to a town to visit, *"the elders of the town trembled at his coming, and said, Comest thou peaceably?"*
1 Samuel 16:4

The reason they asked this is if Samuel was coming to the town in any other mode than peace, they were getting out of town — what he prophesied never failed to come true!

Samuel was an unerring translator between the reality of the spirit and the reality of the natural.

Nothing was lost in the translation — what God intended to be communicated was communicated.

So sure was Samuel of his supernatural eyesight that, when God told him to appoint a successor to king Saul, he was able to discern that, after he had passed all of Jesse's sons, something was wrong:

*"And Samuel said unto Jesse, Are here all thy children? And he said, There remaineth yet the youngest, and, behold, he keepeth the sheep. And Samuel said unto Jesse, **Send and fetch him: for we will not sit down till he come hither.**"*   1 Samuel 16:11

He had seen into the spirit with supernatural eyesight, and he knew that none of the sons he had yet seen was the man who God had called to be king over the land of Israel.

To highlight how impressive that is, as far as Samuel knew, he had seen all of Jesse's sons.

In the natural, he could reasonably assume that he had to choose one of the sons he had seen — as far as he knew, there were no others.

But he was so sure of his supernatural eyesight — so convinced that what he had seen in the spirit was not what he was seeing in the natural — that he felt compelled to ask if there were any sons he had not yet seen.

The prophet's understanding is so clear that he has no doubt of the vision when he is communicating it to the people to whom God has called him to communicate it.

A prophet's life could be difficult, so he had to be absolutely certain that what he was saying had come from the mouth of God.

Samuel's apparent successor, Nathan, had a tremendously difficult task to perform.

The king, David, had committed a heinous crime. He had committed adultery with a man's wife. The woman had conceived a child, and to conceal the crime, David had invited the man — a soldier in his army — back to his home to sleep with his wife.

The idea was that the man, Uriah, would believe the child to be his own and David's sin would be concealed.

Uriah, however, was a patriot, and he refused to be comforted by his wife while his compatriots were still on the battlefield in peril of their lives.

David then decided that there was only one solution to his problem without exposing his sin. He sent Uriah to the front lines of the battle and certain death. As soon as he heard Uriah was dead, David married Uriah's widow and took her into his house so that when she had a child, it would appear to be the legitimate child of David.

His crime was egregious. He had committed murder to conceal another sin, defiling the marriage bed with another man's wife.

Nathan had the difficult task of confronting the king at the word of the Lord:

"And the LORD sent Nathan unto David. And he came unto him, and said unto him, There were two men in one city; the one rich, and the other poor. The rich man had exceeding many flocks and herds: But the poor man had nothing, save one little ewe lamb, which he had bought and nourished up: and it grew up together with him, and with his children; it did eat of his own meat, and drank of

his own cup, and lay in his bosom, and was unto him as a daughter. And there came a traveller unto the rich man, and he spared to take of his own flock and of his own herd, to dress for the wayfaring man that was come unto him; but took the poor man's lamb, and dressed it for the man that was come to him. And David's anger was greatly kindled against the man; and he said to Nathan, As the LORD liveth, the man that hath done this thing shall surely die: And he shall restore the lamb fourfold, because he did this thing, and because he had no pity. And Nathan said to David, **Thou art the man.**"   *2 Samuel 12:1-7*

This is the king of Israel he's talking to!

The prophet who speaks to the king this way had better be sure he has heard the word of God!

Any man who accuses the king of such a heinous crime must be sure that he is righteously accusing the king — if not, he is risking his life!

Prophets were in the old days called "seers," as in "one who sees."

Read that again, because it's revelation.

A prophet is a "seer" — one with SUPER-NATURAL EYESIGHT!

Nathan had to "see" into the spirit and discern what David's crime was and what God wanted him to say to the king.

That is the gist of supernatural eyesight. It is "seeing" into the spirit and reporting what God wants reported.

Another prophet who had to be sure of what he was saying was Elijah the Tishbite, who is unceremoniously introduced to the Bible reader like this:

"And Elijah the Tishbite, who was of the inhabitants of Gilead, said unto Ahab, As the LORD God of Israel liveth, before whom I stand, there shall not be dew nor rain these years, but according to my word."   1 Kings 17:1

This prophet has seen so clearly into the spirit and the supernatural that he is confident saying that rain will only fall when he says it will fall.

Dew will only gather on the ground when he says it will.

Now, rain is one thing, dew is quite another.

Dew forms on the ground as the water vapor in the air condenses and clings to the grass, the ground and other objects.

Elijah pronounced that not only would rain not fall — but dew would also not form on the ground during the time until he would say it would again form.

The prophet had to be sure that he had heard this from the Lord — that his statement was true.

Such was his confidence in the vision God had given him that he was able to pronounce that he himself would be the one whose announcement would bring the rain back.

The role of the prophet is such that the men and women who fill it must be plugged into God — they must be sure of the revelation they are receiving and they must be able to communicate that message effectively to the audience God has called them to communicate it to.

Even when a prophet profoundly dislikes the duty he has been called to do, in his heart, he knows that what God has called him to do is true.

The prophet Jonah, for instance, obviously had supernatural eyesight — he was called to preach to Nineveh, the capital of Assyria, that they were about to be overthrown for their sin.

But Jonah, as a good, patriotic Israelite, **wanted** Nineveh to be overthrown. Assyria was a constant threat to Israel, and it was the hated enemy of his people.

Jonah, who had insight into the spirit, knew that if Nineveh repented at his preaching, God would have mercy on the people there and the city would not be overthrown.

In other words, as a good, patriotic Israelite, Jonah had no desire to see Nineveh repent. He would much rather see them overthrown.

And for awhile, his patriotism wins out — Jonah flees his responsibility:

"Now the word of the LORD came unto Jonah the son of Amittai, saying, Arise, go to Nineveh, that great city, and cry against it; for their wickedness is come up before me. But Jonah rose up to flee unto Tarshish from the presence of the LORD, and went down to Joppa; and he found a ship going to Tarshish: so he paid the fare thereof, and went down into it, to go with them unto Tarshish from the presence of the LORD."   Jonah 1:1-3

His loyalties were with Israel, not with God at that point — mainly because his desire was to see the enemies of Israel perish.

But Jonah knew in his heart that he had to deliver the message God had given him.

When a storm threatens the ship upon which Jonah had escaped, he claims that he fears the Lord and the Lord is the one who has brought about this storm.

We know the story: a giant fish swallows Jonah, and then spits him upon the ground three days later.

Jonah, understanding that he must obey God's call on his life and the things he has seen with supernatural eyesight, goes to Nineveh and preaches.

"But it displeased Jonah exceedingly, and he was very angry. And he prayed unto the LORD, and said, I pray thee, O LORD, was not this my saying, when I was yet in my country? Therefore I fled before unto Tarshish: for I knew that thou art a gracious God, and merciful, slow to anger, and of great kindness, and repentest thee of the evil. Therefore now, O LORD, take, I beseech thee, my life from me; for it is better for me to die than to live. Then said the LORD, Doest thou well to be angry? So Jonah went out of the city, and sat on the east side of the city, and there made him a booth, and sat under it in the shadow, till he might see what would become of the city. And the LORD God prepared a gourd, and made it to come up over Jonah, that it might be a shadow over his head, to deliver him from his grief. So Jonah was exceeding glad of the gourd. But God prepared a worm when the morning rose the next day, and it smote the gourd that it withered. And it came to pass, when the sun did arise, that God prepared a vehement east wind; and the sun beat upon the head of Jonah, that he fainted, and wished in himself to die, and said, It is better for me to die than to live. And God said to Jonah, Doest thou well to be

angry for the gourd? And he said, I do well to be angry,
even unto death. Then said the LORD, Thou hast had pity
on the gourd, for the which thou hast not laboured, neither
madest it grow; which came up in a night, and perished in
a night: And should not I spare Nineveh, that great city,
wherein are more then sixscore thousand persons that
cannot discern between their right hand and their left
hand; and also much cattle?"   *Jonah 4:1-11*

Jonah again talks to God and says, "I told you so! When I was still in Israel, I didn't want to come here because I knew if they repented, You'd have mercy on them."

God uses the metaphor of the gourd to explain to Jonah that, if he could have pity on a plant, God certainly could have pity on an entire city of people who knew no better than to lose themselves in sin.

Even in his disgruntled state, Jonah is taught a tremendous message about God's mercy — that His mercy is not relegated to one nation or one group of people. God is looking for hearts that will turn to Him, not just hearts from one nation.

Supernatural eyesight brings with it a responsibility to learn at the feet of the Lord, even when that lesson may be one that disagrees with everything you have ever believed, as it did with Jonah.

But one prophet stands head and shoulders beyond every other prophet for the depth of his supernatural eyesight — the breadth of his understanding of God and His nature.

That prophet, of course, is John the Baptist, about whom Jesus said, *"Verily I say unto you, Among them that are*

*born of women there hath not risen a greater than John
the Baptist."*   *Matthew 11:11*

John the Baptist was the prophet who prepared the way
for Jesus.

His role in life was to prepare Israel for the advent of its
Messiah. He was the one who called the nation to repent,
told the king of the nation that his relationship was unholy.

And he was the one who pronounced that Jesus was "the
Lamb of God, who takes away the sins of the world."

His supernatural eyesight was so pervasive, so all-
present in his life, that while he was yet in his mother's
womb, he rejoiced in the presence of God as Jesus
approached, also in his mother's womb.

Such supernatural eyesight is clearly in the Old
Testament and the early New Testament the role of
prophets — those specifically called to peer into the
supernatural and relay the message found there to those
who are solidly living in the natural.

But with the death, burial and resurrection of Jesus
Christ, the Holy Spirit made His home in men, and the
nature of God's relationship with mankind fundamentally
changed — making all believers "kings and priests."

CHAPTER 6

DAVID — THE SHEPHERD'S SECRET TO REVELATION

We cannot talk about supernatural eyesight without talking about a man who the Bible says is a *"man after God's own heart."*   *1 Samuel 13:14*

David was a shepherd. He spent long hours tending the sheep of his father, playing music on his harp, meditating on God and praying.

That experience alone with God forged an incredible and deep love of God in David's heart.

That love bred an ever-deepening relationship with God that took David into incredible revelatory depths with God and a supernatural understanding of God's nature that few other people have ever matched.

Our first example in the Bible of David's extraordinary understanding of God comes in one of the most famous stories about his life.

"And there went out a champion out of the camp of the Philistines, named Goliath, of Gath, whose height was six cubits and a span. And he had an helmet of brass upon his head, and he was armed with a coat of mail; and the weight of the coat was five thousand shekels of brass. And he had greaves of brass upon his legs, and a target of brass between his shoulders. And the staff of his spear was like a weaver's beam; and his spear's head weighed six hundred shekels of iron: and one bearing a shield went before him. And he stood and cried unto the armies of

Israel, and said unto them, Why are ye come out to set
your battle in array? am not I a Philistine, and ye servants
to Saul? choose you a man for you, and let him come
down to me. If he be able to fight with me, and to kill me,
then will we be your servants: but if I prevail against him,
and kill him, then shall ye be our servants, and serve us.
And the Philistine said, I defy the armies of Israel this
day; give me a man, that we may fight together. When Saul
and all Israel heard those words of the Philistine, they
were dismayed, and greatly afraid."   *1 Samuel 17:4-11*

This massive man, Goliath, is estimated to have stood
about nine feet tall. His imposing figure sent terror down
the spines of the Israelites who faced him — none was
confident in their abilities to face this man and defeat him.

And, in the natural, they were right to be afraid. He was
the champion of the Philistines. He was a battle-hardened
warrior who had every natural advantage over all the men
of Israel.

Their fear of him — in the natural — was prudent and wise.

In the natural, his challenge to them was a military challenge.

But there was one young man in Israel who had looked
beyond the natural. While the entire nation was looking at
the logistical challenges of facing such an imposing and
overwhelmingly powerful foe, one young man was
looking deep into the supernatural by the power of God
and seeing the reality — that Goliath's challenge was not
natural at all; it was a supernatural challenge.

"And David left his carriage in the hand of the keeper of
the carriage, and ran into the army, and came and saluted
his brethren. And as he talked with them, behold, there
came up the champion, the Philistine of Gath, Goliath by

name, out of the armies of the Philistines, and spake according to the same words: and David heard them. And all the men of Israel, when they saw the man, fled from him, and were sore afraid. And the men of Israel said, Have ye seen this man that is come up? surely to defy Israel is he come up: and it shall be, that the man who killeth him, the king will enrich him with great riches, and will give him his daughter, and make his father's house free in Israel. And David spake to the men that stood by him, saying, What shall be done to the man that killeth this Philistine, and taketh away the reproach from Israel? for **who is this uncircumcised Philistine, that he should defy the armies of the living God?"** *1 Samuel 17:22-26*

David's question had nothing to do with the Philistine's qualifications to wage battle — those were clear to anyone who looked at him.

David was not interested in acquiring weapons sufficient to slay the giant — he understood, by his supernatural eyesight, that the challenge of the Philistine was supernatural.

He understood that the Philistine was not challenging the armies of Israel — he was challenging their God.

In his mind, it was impossible to believe that nobody had yet slain the giant and taken the reproach away from Israel — how is it that this Philistine has such power to continue to defy the armies of the living God?

Just as Jesus, when he encountered disbelief among his disciples, seemed shocked and disappointed by the reality that their faith was not strong, David finds it hard to believe that there is not one man in Israel who has gone out and given himself to be God's instrument of judgment on this insolent Philistine.

This is another aspect of those who have supernatural eyesight — they understand that *every physical manifestation has an underlying spiritual cause or root.*

The universe itself is one tremendous manifestation of the underlying spiritual cause — that God commanded it to be.

The Philistine's challenge had an underlying spiritual cause — that the Philistines had no respect for the God of Israel.

This is also the place where David demonstrates the character that makes him Israel's greatest king.

Saul, who was a head taller than the rest of the Israelites, was the technical king at this time, but if he had been a real leader of the people, he would have taken the Philistine's challenge personally and would have gone out himself in faith and vanquished the challenger.

But David — barely more than a boy — showed the leadership that nobody else in Israel had. He stepped forward to lead the nation in both physical and spiritual exploits as he accepted the challenge from the giant. As he stepped out into the battlefield, David again demonstrated that he had a firm grasp of God's principles:

" And the Philistine said unto David, Am I a dog, that thou comest to me with staves? And the Philistine cursed David by his gods. And the Philistine said to David, Come to me, and I will give thy flesh unto the fowls of the air, and to the beasts of the field. Then said David to the Philistine, **Thou comest to me with a sword, and with a spear, and with a shield: but I come to thee in the name of the LORD of hosts, the God of the armies of Israel, whom thou hast defied.** *This day will the LORD deliver thee into mine hand; and I will smite thee, and take thine*

head from thee; and I will give the carcases of the host of the Philistines this day unto the fowls of the air, and to the wild beasts of the earth; **that all the earth may know that there is a God in Israel. And all this assembly shall know that the LORD saveth not with sword and spear:** *for the battle is the LORD's, and he will give you into our hands."*

1 Samuel 17:43-47

This was a basic struggle between flesh and spirit.

The Philistine looked in the natural at a young man with no weapons of war and couldn't believe that *this* was the champion of Israel. But David was looking in the spirit — he understood that, no matter how many weapons of war the Philistine brought, he could not prevail against the God who had created the universe.

While it seems simple to us using hindsight to see that David did indeed win the battle with nothing more than a sling and a smooth stone, it was another thing entirely for him in the moment. After all, he was facing what possibly was the largest man he had ever seen, battle-hardened and belligerent.

The mighty men of the armies of Israel were afraid of this massive man.

So for us, it's easy to say, "Oh, yeah. Everyone should have known that the battle was the Lord's." It's easy to say that from the safe distance of about 3,000 years.

But it's another thing when you're staring down the barrel of a spear that looks like a weaver's beam with a 9-foot tall battle-hardened warrior shouting that he's going to kill you and feed your carcass to the wild animals.

For David to face down this immediate threat of death, he had absolute trust in the spiritual truths he had learned while singing to the Lord and praying as he shepherded his father's flocks.

But his prowess as a God-believing warrior was not the only aspect of David's character that showed the awesome power of God to form a man in His image.

Shortly after David's battle over Goliath, one of the most awesome displays of God's love exhibiting in someone's life comes to light in the Bible:

I Samuel 18 says something fascinating: *"And it happened, when he finished speaking to Saul, the soul of Jonathan was knitted with the soul of David; and Jonathan loved him as his own soul."*   *1 Samuel 18:1*

Jonathan and David's souls were knitted — they were exhibiting the love between brothers that Jesus later admonished people who truly loved God to exhibit.

That's a very vivid word picture. It means the very core of Jonathan's soul was weaved together with David's. This picture is deeper than we realize. This relationship was deeper than most of our relationships today can hope to be.

Many people today never have any friends they could say their soul was knitted to.

They have close friends, but they hold back part of themselves — there's always some part that is protected, unavailable to the friend.

They never could share their deepest fears and pains. They couldn't share the core of their being with their friends.

But the picture painted by the book of 1 Samuel is one of two men who completely open themselves up, and whose souls are knitted together.

The Bible continues: *"And Jonathan and David cut a covenant, because he loved him as his own soul. And Jonathan stripped himself of the robe that was on him, and gave it to David; also his apparel, even to his sword and to his bow and his belt."*   *Verses 3-4*

Jonathan said, *"take the sign of who I am — my robe — it's yours. Take my covering and put it on you. Take all my weapons. All my power. Everything that identifies me as who I am — it's yours."*

He's saying, *"there are no barriers between us. I am completely defenseless against you. You have the weapons. I have none. I am vulnerable to you."*

True love is vulnerable.

True love has no defense against the one it loves. If David had chosen to take the sword and thrust it into Jonathan's chest, Jonathan would have had no defense. He would have just stood there and died.

That kind of vulnerability is a figure for us to understand the trust these two men had between themselves.

True love makes no effort to defend itself.

We so often don't love like we could because we're too busy defending ourselves against those we claim to love.

We're too busy coming up with a way to survive when the person we supposedly love fails us — we plan for the failure of our supposed love.

And it usually fails because we have doomed it from the start by not being vulnerable. We're so busy protecting ourselves that there's no way we can possibly give ourselves to the one we're supposed to be loving.

So from the start, Jonathan and David's relationship was built on intimacy — on being completely open and vulnerable to each other. If you hurt me, David, I guess I'll just have to be hurt. I guess I'll just have to suffer, because I don't have any kind of wall built against you. I don't have a shield protecting me from you. You have complete access to my heart. My soul is knitted to yours.

In a sense, Jonathan and David were laying down their lives for each other.

They were putting their lives on the line and giving the other man complete control.

That love comes as a result of someone who has looked deep into the deep things of God and has been changed by his supernatural vision into God's character. Remember, Moses was willing to lay his own salvation on the line to secure the salvation of the children of Israel.

Indeed, the love Jonathan and David shared was so pure that David recognized it was extravagant. When Jonathan died, David said: *"I am distressed over you, my brother Jonathan. You were very delightful to me; your love was wonderful to me, more than the love of women."*

2 Samuel 1:26

There was something pure about it that engraved in David's mind the truth of it — that the love he shared with Jonathan was true love; it wasn't romantic love...

It wasn't just love between brothers...

It wasn't just love between friends.

It was all-consuming, laying down your life, holy love that stems from a heart that is completely given to be open and engulfed in the spirit of God you see inside another person.

There is gratification in loving people of the opposite sex.

There is gratification in loving your friends.

But David and Jonathan shared a love that went layers and layers beyond those surface loves that we all seem to engulf ourselves in.

They shared a completely vulnerable love, a completely open and self-sacrificing love that many can only dream of ever sharing with someone else on this earth.

More relevant for us, however, is what the love of Jonathan and David can tell us about the love of God — and their ability to, through the Spirit discern that and allow it to be manifested in their lives.

We often think God's first expression of love toward us was in the action of conceiving of and creating us. In other words, we think God's love was manifested first to us through His very act of creation.

And on one level that's true — He loved all His creation.

But on a deeper, more intimate level, God's first act of love toward us was opening Himself up to us and allowing us to hurt Him.

It was making a creation that could rebel against Him and reject Him even after it had full knowledge of who He is.

David innately understood that love and exhibited it in his own life for the rest of his life.

When Saul sought his life, David refused to stretch out his hand to take the life of Saul.

When his own son sought to usurp him from the kingdom, David refused to take action against him because the love of God was, as the Bible says, *"shed abroad"* in *his heart.*   *Romans 5:5*

David had a profound revelation of God's holiness, His love and His power that were forged by days, weeks, months and years alone with God on the fields as the herds grazed.

"The heavens declare the glory of God; and the firmament sheweth his handywork. Day unto day uttereth speech, and night unto night sheweth knowledge. [There is] no speech nor language, [where] their voice is not heard. Their line is gone out through all the earth, and their words to the end of the world. In them hath he set a tabernacle for the sun, Which [is] as a bridegroom coming out of his chamber, [and] rejoiceth as a strong man to run a race. His going forth [is] from the end of the heaven, and his circuit unto the ends of it: and there is nothing hid from the heat thereof. The law of the LORD [is] perfect, converting the soul: the testimony of the LORD [is] sure, making wise the simple."   *Psalm 19:1-7*

As he stood on the fields, gazing up at the heavens, the stars, the clouds, the deep blue of the sky during the summer days, you can almost imagine David watching the glory of God's creation and marveling at the Hand that had wrought it.

David says the skies are actually a witness — as in a witness in court — that testifies, "Hey, God made me!"

As he gazes up to the sky, David has a profound understanding that, no matter where a man goes on the planet, to hear a testimony of God's power and His immenseness, all the man has to do is look up to the sky and pages and pages of testimony will begin to unfold before their very eyes.

You can just imagine David, awestruck at the majesty of God, crying out to Him in song, "the heavens declare your glory!"

David was a shepherd; he had nothing but time on his hands to stare up into the skies, try to count the stars and understand how big God had to be to make the massive thing he was staring at.

He had nothing but time to commune with God, to spend time getting to know the one who called Himself "self-existent."

As he looked to the daytime sky, he heard the majesty of God in the peals of thunder, in the gentle pelting of the rain, in the chirps of the crickets, in the gentle breath of the wind. As he got closer and closer to God, he began to see the fingerprints of God on everything around him. He began to see the beauty of the rock that had never been chiseled by human hands, the genius of the simple plant that, despite its simplicity, could take the light of the sun and convert it into food for man and animal to eat.

Did you ever think of that?

When you eat, in a very real way, you are eating the sun!

The sun literally spits out pieces of itself that hurtle to earth in about eight minutes. Those pieces of itself then find their way to the leaves of plants, which through photosynthesis convert the pieces of the sun into cells that animals later eat and store as energy.

David had little to do but sit around and contemplate these questions and marvel at the awesomeness of the God who had created a world that worked just the way ours does.

No wonder that, when he picked up his harp and began to sing, the words that flowed from his mouth were "The universe records Your splendor, the sky boldly proclaims the work of Your hands. ...Each and every day gushes forth testimony, and each and every night lives your knowledge."

This psalm is a love song from David to God; it is an uncontrived outpouring of wonder, amazement and love toward the Creator of the Universe.

But David's wonderment at God's power did not stop there.

In Psalm 8, he asked the question that is on everyone's mind who considers the magnitude of God:

"O LORD our Lord, how excellent [is] thy name in all the earth! who hast set thy glory above the heavens. Out of the mouth of babes and sucklings hast thou ordained strength because of thine enemies, that thou mightest still the enemy and the avenger. When I consider thy heavens, the work of thy fingers, the moon and the stars, which thou hast ordained; What is man, that thou art mindful of him? and the son of man, that thou visitest him?" Psalm 8:1-4

How excellent is your name, Jehovah, the self-existent One! No wonder the babies magnify your name. No wonder you have established strength!

When I think about the heavens, the expanse and the incredible bodies it contains — the stars and the moon — I think about your magnitude; I think about how large and awesome you are.

And then I start to think, "I am so small, I am just a man who is just a speck on the earth."

Remember, when Saul was about to promote David, David said, I am the youngest son of my father, the lowest man in the tribe of Benjamin, the lowliest tribe in the nation.

David was keenly aware that the earth did not revolve around him; he understood that he was small, and in the eyes of the world, insignificant.

But as he sat on the field, watching the sheep, wondering in awe at the work of God in space and the sky, he started to feel even smaller when he understood the sheer magnitude of a God who could create all that.

And then his wonder gushed out of his belly as he wondered in song, "I am a nobody; who am I that God should pay attention to me, or visit me?"

His wonder was the expression of the understanding — gained through supernatural eyesight — that God, even though He is huge beyond our imagining and powerful beyond the human mind's capability to comprehend, has chosen to not only interact with man, but has made man "a little lower than the angels," or as the Hebrew says, "a little less than God," meaning perhaps that it is amazing that *God has exalted lowly man to the place of friend.*

When we think of these incredible things, it is both humbling and awe inspiring that God would not only listen to our prayers, but that he would even care enough to count the hairs on our heads.

So at the end of this, David comes to a conclusion:

"The fear of the LORD [is] clean, enduring for ever: the judgments of the LORD [are] true [and] righteous altogether. More to be desired [are they] than gold, yea, than much fine gold: sweeter also than honey and the honeycomb. Moreover by them is thy servant warned: [and] in keeping of them [there is] great reward. Who can understand [his] errors? cleanse thou me from secret [faults]. Keep back thy servant also from presumptuous [sins]; let them not have dominion over me: then shall I be upright, and I shall be innocent from the great transgression. Let the words of my mouth, and the meditation of my heart, be acceptable in thy sight, O LORD, my strength, and my redeemer."   *Psalm 19:9-14*

With such a big, impressive and awesome God, whose judgments are always true, what good would gold do me? I want the judgments, the spiritual direction, of God. You can't buy that kind of access. It's worth more than all the money you can accumulate.

His judgments are sweeter than honey.

David is pleading for God to direct him, to lead him, through an incredibly personal relationship, every step of his life.

Is it any wonder that God called him "a man after my own heart?"

And then David makes the cry that essentially is what Jesus preached for three years:

"Let the words of my mouth AND THE MEDITATIONS OF MY HEART be acceptable in thy sight, O Lord."

When you achieve supernatural eyesight, you begin, as David, to look around the natural world and be filled with wonder at the God who framed all of it — you understand all things in a spiritual context.

You understand that the sky is there to testify of God's glory.

You understand that the day itself preaches His Gospel.

You understand that God's greatest desire for our lives is to manifest His presence in our lives so that our very thoughts and meditations are pleasing to Him.

That, partner, is supernatural eyesight.

But David's profound understanding of truths in the spirit does not just stop with military power, with understanding of the love of God or with the natural world that testifies of God's glory.

David had a profound understanding also of the Scriptures that God had preached, and how the Law was to be interpreted.

"Then came David to Nob to Ahimelech the priest: and Ahimelech was afraid at the meeting of David, and said unto him, Why art thou alone, and no man with thee? And David said unto Ahimelech the priest, The king hath commanded me a business, and hath said unto me, Let no man know any thing of the business whereabout I send thee, and what I have commanded thee: and I have appointed my servants to such and such a place. Now therefore what is under thine hand? give me five loaves of

*bread in mine hand, or what there is present. And the
priest answered David, and said, There is no common
bread under mine hand, but there is hallowed bread; if the
young men have kept themselves at least from women.* **And
David answered the priest, and said unto him, Of a truth
women have been kept from us about these three days,
since I came out, and the vessels** *of the young men are
holy, and the bread is in a manner common, yea, though it
were sanctified this day in the vessel. So the priest gave
him hallowed bread: for there was no bread there but the
shewbread, that was taken from before the LORD, to put
hot bread in the day when it was taken away."*

1 Samuel 21:1-6

David's understanding of the nature of God helped him
understand the Scripture in the manner it was intended to
be interpreted. Though the Law forbade David from eating
the shewbread, David innately — through his
understanding of God gained through his intimacy with
Him — that the Law was given for man.

In fact, Jesus later commended him for his actions:

*"But he said unto them, Have ye not read what David
did, when he was an hungred, and they that were with
him;* **How he entered into the house of God, and did eat
the shewbread, which was not lawful for him to eat,**
*neither for them which were with him, but only for the
priests? Or have ye not read in the law, how that on the
sabbath days the priests in the temple profane the sabbath,
and are blameless?"*

Matthew 12:3-5

Jesus commended David for his understanding of the
Law — that the law was made for man; man was not
made for the Law.

David understood this truth because he had spent his time digging deeper, always seeking to know more of God and to know God more.

As you read the rest of this book, understand that is one of the most important keys to supernatural eyesight: never being satisfied that you have "arrived."

CHAPTER 7

STONING CAN'T STOP THE REVELATION (THE WOMAN WITH THE ISSUE OF BLOOD)

There's a Scripture in the New Testament that exemplifies the attitude of those who have supernatural eyesight.

A woman who is overtaken with a heinous disease has come to the end of her rope.

As she considers her options, she sees deep into the spirit to understand that the cure to the disease that has ailed her for a dozen years is walking down the street:

"And a certain woman, which had an issue of blood twelve years, And had suffered many things of many physicians, and had spent all that she had, and was nothing bettered, but rather grew worse, When she had heard of Jesus, came in the press behind, and touched his garment. For she said, If I may touch but his clothes, I shall be whole. And straightway the fountain of her blood was dried up; and she felt in her body that she was healed of that plague. And Jesus, immediately knowing in himself that virtue had gone out of him, turned him about in the press, and said, Who touched my clothes? And his disciples said unto him, Thou seest the multitude thronging thee, and sayest thou, Who touched me? And he looked round about to see her that had done this thing. But the woman fearing and trembling, knowing what was done in her, came and

fell down before him, and told him all the truth. And he said unto her, Daughter, thy faith hath made thee whole; go in peace, and be whole of thy plague."

Mark 5:25-34

The context of this scripture is telling.

The woman had come to the end of herself — she could no longer believe in the methods of the physical world to take care of her problem. She had tried everything she was supposed to try.

She had "suffered many things" at the hands of the doctors of her day...

She had spent all her money on trying to find a cure to the disease that had plagued her for more than a decade, but men were unable to help her at all.

The Law delivered by Moses prescribed that she was not to be in the midst of the people — because of her continual issue of blood, she was unclean and to be quarantined.

To be found in the midst of people could have meant stoning to the woman — dying by having rocks thrown at her until her body stopped functioning. Stoning is a very unpleasant way to die, and that was the penalty that awaited this woman if she was found in the midst of people.

But she had tried everything else. She had tried doctors, she had spent all her money — no physical help could change her situation.

The Bible does not tell us how she heard of Jesus, but it's likely that she heard of Him the same way so many others did: by word of mouth.

His fame was part of what the religious leaders of his day feared — the people regarded Him as a prophet and some rightly regarded Him as the Messiah. Everywhere He went, the people whispered and spread stories of the tremendous miracles that followed Him from place to place.

As he entered a city, doubtlessly the whispers would begin flying:

"Did you hear He raised a dead girl?"

"I heard He cast the devils out of the maniac in Gadarenes."

"Someone said He commanded the weather — and the weather obeyed Him."

"The temple priests themselves saw that Jesus healed a man who was blind from birth — something that's never been done before."

The woman with the issue of blood certainly would have heard the rumors — perhaps from a longtime friend who had suffered alongside her. Perhaps she heard from someone running through the streets, shouting that the Lord was nigh.

However she heard about Him, the woman with the issue of blood had a tremendous thing happen inside herself as soon as she heard.

Her hearing brought belief.

The Bible gives us a specific flow of events in the journey of faith in the human spirit:

"So then faith cometh by hearing, and hearing by the word of God." Romans 10:17

This woman heard the word, and then the hearing of the word brought faith in her — her supernatural eyesight was awakened.

She had come to the end of herself — she had nothing left to lose by trying to reach the Lord and receive her healing.

Now, the woman with the issue of blood had to die. Maybe you don't understand the death that this woman had to really make. Being a Jew, living under the law, she had a sickness and a disease that she was not allowed to touch anybody when she walked down the street. If she touched anybody, she could be stoned.

In the midst of a tremendous crowd, she was forbidden from touching anyone else. She was commanded to stay completely away by the traditions of the elders.

But *she had to die to her tradition.*

She said: "I'm going to get what I hear that this man has the ability to give me, even if I have to potentially face stoning or death."

The natural things told her she had no hope…

The natural things told her to give up and just settle for her lot in life, to let her situation dictate her actions.

But she refused.

Now, this woman wasn't a quack. She wasn't someone who took every sickness to alternative medicine. She had gone to the doctors. The fact of the matter is that she spent all the money she had.

What do you do when you have done everything you can do? Do you give up? Do you say there is no hope? No, you don't! You don't give up, you look up!

By coming to the end of herself, she let go of any claims the flesh had to a solution to her problem.

Now, there's nothing wrong with going to a doctor for a sickness — I believe God has anointed doctors to learn about the human condition and use their God-given knowledge to help us when they can.

But there are places doctors can't go, and things they can't do, even with all their advanced technology.

A doctor can diagnose your cancer, he can flood your body with radiation (killing both good and bad cells) and fill you full of chemicals designed to actually kill you — though in the smaller doses, they're supposed to only kill the cancer.

A doctor can diagnose Human Immunodeficiency Virus (the virus that causes AIDS), and with drug "cocktails," he can slow down the diseases march to your death, but in the end, he is powerless to defeat the disease.

Doctors are good for the purposes they serve — but they have limits.

This woman had reached that limit — there was nothing else the doctors could do for her.

Every claim the flesh had to her healing had been relinquished — the flesh had admitted that it didn't have the answers; this woman would have to settle to die if she was depending on the flesh for her answers.

But when she heard the word that the Healer was in town…

When she heard He was traveling through, her hearing provoked supernatural eyesight within her bosom — her faith woke up, stood at attention and said to her, "GET TO THE MASTER, WHATEVER YOU HAVE TO DO TO GET THERE!"

She was no longer concerned about what rules she might have to break to get there — remember, she was forbidden from being around people.

She was no longer concerned about the physical consequences of her actions — after all, she was a walking dead woman anyway!

Nothing was going to stand in her way; not rules, not threats, and certainly not the massive crowd that gathered around Jesus.

This woman was not interested in monopolizing Jesus' time — she was not interested in trying to impress Him with her faith.

Read that again.

She did not try to impress the Lord with how much she believed. She, in fact, did not want attention at all — all she wanted was what she firmly believed she could get from Him: healing.

Many times, those who believe less than they know they could seek out a man of God and try to engage in long, theological discussions to highlight their grasp of the Bible and its message.

Some of the Pharisees tried to do this with Jesus.

They tried to gain his implicit approval for the condition of their lives as they were — they were not interested in changing by receiving His message. Instead, they wanted Him to tell them they were OK just like they were.

Take this nugget of truth deep into your own spirit: Everyone is the hero of their own story.

If every natural person on the planet wrote a story from the depths of their being, the main character, the hero, would be them. (Those in the Spirit would write of Jesus, but the NATURAL people would write a story about themselves).

Every person perceives themselves in the best light possible — nobody wants to think ill of themselves. So it was natural for the Pharisees and religious people to seek praise for themselves as they were, without changing. After all, in their own perception, they were doing the best they could.

In the church, many are the same way. Nobody thinks they have as much growing to do as they actually do.

So they seek out the pastor or the pastor's wife, or the evangelist to have a long conversation with them and impress them with the depth of their knowledge and faith.

But this woman was not interested in winning praise.

She was not interested in a self-esteem boosting affirmation of her faith. Such a pat on the back could have done her no good, anyway.

Her problem was not a lack of self-esteem; her problem was she couldn't stop bleeding!

So the woman did not seek an audience with Jesus. She didn't even seek acknowledgement from Him. In fact, she didn't even want Him to notice her at all. She simply knew that He was the One with the power.

She knew that He was the one who had opened the blind eyes, unstopped the mute mouths, made the deaf ears hear, the cripple walk and the dead rise.

She knew that if she could just touch part of Him, if she could just reach out and graze the hem of His garment, she would be healed, and that was all that was important to her at that moment.

She had a supernatural understanding that He was the Son of the living God.

And she could not have reached that understanding without supernatural eyesight:

"He saith unto them, But whom say ye that I am? And Simon Peter answered and said, Thou art the Christ, the Son of the living God. And Jesus answered and said unto him, Blessed art thou, Simon Barjona: **for flesh and blood hath not revealed it unto thee,** *but my Father which is in heaven."*
Matthew 16:15-17

And again, Jesus made it clear:

"No man can come to me, except the Father which hath sent me draw him: and I will raise him up at the last day. It is written in the prophets, And they shall be all taught of God. Every man therefore that hath heard, and hath learned of the Father, cometh unto me."
John 6:44-45

Supernatural eyesight has its beginning when a man or woman is learning of God — when He is revealing His Son to them and that He is who He says He is and He'll do what He says He'll do.

Faith comes by that hearing!

This woman had that faith because the Father drew her — she could not have come to Him in the true faith she exhibited otherwise!

When she had pressed through the crowd — I can't stress enough how dangerous for her that was — she saw an opportunity to touch the hem of His garment. She reached out and just brushed the bottom of His garment.

And, though He was being pushed from every side by the massive crowd that had gathered to see Him, when she had touched Him, her simple, rock-solid faith got His attention.

It's often overlooked that, in the midst of this incredible crowd, in the midst of all the people who were touching Him, only ONE person touched Him with faith that made Him take notice!

Remember the last portion of the scripture that started out this chapter:

*"And Jesus, immediately knowing in himself that virtue had gone out of him, turned him about in the press, and said, Who touched my clothes? **And his disciples said unto him, Thou seest the multitude thronging thee, and sayest thou, Who touched me?** And he looked round about to see her that had done this thing. But the woman fearing and trembling, knowing what was done in her, came and fell down*

before him, and told him all the truth. And he said unto her, Daughter, thy faith hath made thee whole; go in peace, and be whole of thy plague."

In the midst of the multitude, only ONE TOUCH got His attention, because only ONE TOUCH was done in pure faith!

The woman, understanding that she had been healed by His power, trembled in His presence, and she spilled the beans; "It was I who touched you!"

Supernatural eyesight is the ability to see beyond the natural and see the truth in the Spirit.

It is the ability that this woman exhibited to, after years of failure seeing doctors, believe that there is a Holy God who can heal.

Supernatural eyesight is the difference between someone praying for you and just flapping their jaws and someone praying for you in faith and receiving the answer to prayer!

Supernatural eyesight is seeing past the natural reality. In the natural reality, cancer can't be healed. In the natural reality, AIDS is a death sentence. In the natural reality, all manner of diseases are impossible to heal.

But those who can peer past the flesh, past the natural and into the Spirit understand that the God who created it all is more than able to change the natural into His will.

Supernatural eyesight is the ability to see that and believe it.

Anyone can believe with "head knowledge" that Jesus is a healer. But the person who sees with supernatural eyesight is the one who has "heart knowledge" that He really IS a healer.

The woman with the issue of blood was such a person. We hear nothing else of her in the Bible, but it's certain that she went on to an incredible life in Christ — her faith was solid and unshakeable.

CHAPTER 8:

PAUL — THE APOSTLE OF SUPERNATURAL INSIGHT INTO GOD'S WORD

Paul was a master of the Law. He was a "Pharisee of Pharisees." He was a student of Gamaliel. He was clearly a leader of his day at the Law of Moses. Through his letters, we see that Paul had a masterful command of the Scriptures.

In fact, one of Paul's letters goes into great detail listing his credentials in handling the Law:

"Though I might also have confidence in the flesh. If any other man thinketh that he hath whereof he might trust in the flesh, I more: Circumcised the eighth day, of the stock of Israel, of the tribe of Benjamin, an Hebrew of the Hebrews; as touching the law, a Pharisee; Concerning zeal, persecuting the church; touching the righteousness which is in the law, blameless. But what things were gain to me, those I counted loss for Christ. Yea doubtless, and I count all things but loss for the excellency of the knowledge of Christ Jesus my Lord: for whom I have suffered the loss of all things, and do count them but dung, that I may win Christ."   *Philippians 3:4-11*

Peter and the rest of the apostles, on the other hand, were not masters of the Law; they were fishermen, tax collectors and such. Each had his place and understanding in the Gospel.

But it was the master of the Law — Paul — who preached, time after time, salvation by grace, grace, grace.

It was the fisherman, Peter, who at least once sought to put the Greek converts to Christianity under the Law of the Jews in the matters of circumcision and the dietary laws.

The master of the Law was advocating freedom from it, and the Galilean fisherman was advocating adherence to the Law. The Bible tells us that Peter was wrong.

Here's what Paul says: "But when Peter came to Antioch, I opposed him to his face, because he was to be blamed. For before some came from James, he ate with the Gentiles. But when they came, he drew back and separated himself, being afraid of (the Jews). And also the rest of the Jews dissembled with him, so as even Barnabas was led away with their dissembling. But when I saw that they did not walk uprightly with the truth of the gospel, I said to Peter before all, If you being a Jew live as a Gentile, and not as the Jews, why do you compel the Gentiles to Judaize?" Galatians 2:11-14

How did Paul, who was raised on the Law and who was zealous for the Law, come to such a complete turnaround in the Christian church? It was supernatural eyesight!

Peter believed that people are saved by grace, but when the Jews came around, he changed his story!

Paul spent the vast majority of his ministry dealing with that problem. When he was writing to the church at Colosse, he said:

"Watch that there be not one robbing you through philosophy and empty deceit, according to the tradition of men, according to the elements of this world, and not

*according to Christ. For in Him dwells all the fullness of
the Godhead bodily; and having been filled, you are in
Him, who is the head of all rule and authority..."*

Colossians 2:8-10

Paul warns the church to beware, because otherwise
someone will ROB them.

Someone will steal something from them through
philosophy and lies — lies that are formed according to
the tradition of men.

This is important.

Paul says someone will deceive them by teaching them
the traditions of men.

*He's echoing the words of Jesus: "For laying aside
the commandment of God, ye (keep) the tradition of
men, as the washing of pots and cups: and many other
such like things ye do. And he said unto them, Full well
ye reject the commandment of God, that ye may keep
your own tradition."*   *Mark 7:8-9*

Paul refers to the traditions of men when he says that
the people who seek to teach them to you are seeking to
rob you.

He says Jesus is the head of all rule and authority —
He's in charge of those who are in charge; He's got
authority more than the rules of the Law. He is the Head
of them all.

Remember, this is the master of the Law saying this;
this is Paul, who made his reputation by knowing and
being zealous for the Law. Now he's saying that Jesus has

authority over the Law, and those who try to get you to follow traditions of man are thieves.

How did Paul come by such tremendous understanding? To find out, we must go to his calling:

"And Saul, yet breathing out threatenings and slaughter against the disciples of the Lord, went unto the high priest, And desired of him letters to Damascus to the synagogues, that if he found any of this way, whether they were men or women, he might bring them bound unto Jerusalem. And as he journeyed, he came near Damascus: and suddenly there shined round about him a light from heaven: And he fell to the earth, and heard a voice saying unto him, Saul, Saul, why persecutest thou me? And he said, Who art thou, Lord? And the Lord said, I am Jesus whom thou persecutest: it is hard for thee to kick against the pricks. And he trembling and astonished said, Lord, what wilt thou have me to do? And the Lord said unto him, Arise, and go into the city, and it shall be told thee what thou must do. And the men which journeyed with him stood speechless, hearing a voice, but seeing no man. And Saul arose from the earth; and when his eyes were opened, he saw no man: but they led him by the hand, and brought him into Damascus. And he was three days without sight, and neither did eat nor drink." Acts 9:1-9

In the spirit, we can see that Paul's physical blindness was a manifestation of his spiritual blindness. Remember, all truth is parallel. Paul was blinded in the physical to make a statement about his condition in the spiritual.

"And Ananias went his way, and entered into the house; and putting his hands on him said, Brother Saul, the Lord, even Jesus, that appeared unto thee in the way as thou camest, hath sent me, that thou mightest receive thy sight,

and be filled with the Holy Ghost. **And immediately there fell from his eyes as it had been scales:** *and he received sight forthwith, and arose, and was baptized.* **And when he had received meat, he was strengthened. Then was Saul certain days with the disciples which were at Damascus. And straightway he preached Christ in the synagogues,** *that he is the Son of God."* Acts 9:17-20

The physical scales falling from Paul's eyes were the physical manifestation of the truth that was happening in the spiritual — Paul, though he was a learned master of the Law, finally UNDERSTOOD!

When the scales fell from his spiritual eyes, he had SUPERNATURAL EYESIGHT!

He even later says as much:

"And not as Moses, which put a vail over his face, that the children of Israel could not stedfastly look to the end of that which is abolished: But their minds were blinded: **for until this day remaineth the same vail untaken away in the reading of the old testament;** *which vail is done away in Christ. But even unto this day, when Moses is read, the vail is upon their heart. Nevertheless when it shall turn to the Lord, the vail shall be taken away. Now the Lord is that Spirit: and where the Spirit of the Lord is, there is liberty. But we all, with open face beholding as in a glass the glory of the Lord, are changed into the same image from glory to glory, even as by the Spirit of the Lord."*
2 Corinthians 3:13-18

As far as Paul was concerned, he understood that, until they received supernatural eyesight by being redeemed by Christ, those who read the Old Testament were prevented from supernatural revelation by the same veil that covered Moses' face when he came down from the presence of God.

The same veil prevented them from seeing into the spirit and understanding the revelation truths God had for them there.

Paul's understanding into the nature of God instantly became so profound that those who opposed him feared his understanding and his prowess at interpreting the Word of God with such incredible insight.

In fact, when he was testifying, Paul's ability to see into the spirit and pull out truth for the world today — as the prophets, to translate the spirit into the natural — inspired awe in those around him:

*"Having therefore obtained help of God, I continue unto this day, witnessing both to small and great, saying none other things than those which the prophets and Moses did say should come: That Christ should suffer, and that he should be the first that should rise from the dead, and should shew light unto the people, and to the Gentiles. And as he thus spake for himself, **Festus said with a loud voice, Paul, thou art beside thyself; much learning doth make thee mad.** But he said, I am not mad, most noble Festus; but speak forth the words of truth and soberness. For the king knoweth of these things, before whom also I speak freely: for I am persuaded that none of these things are hidden from him; for this thing was not done in a corner. King Agrippa, believest thou the prophets? I know that thou believest. Then Agrippa said unto Paul, Almost thou persuadest me to be a Christian. And Paul said, I would to God, that not only thou, but also all that hear me this day, were both almost, and altogether such as I am, except these bonds. And when he had thus spoken, the king rose up, and the governor, and Bernice, and they that sat with them: And when they were gone aside, they talked*

between themselves, saying, This man doeth nothing worthy of death or of bonds."   *Acts 26:22-31*

Paul's understanding of the Word was so profound, so God-inspired, that hearing it, the natural man could not comprehend it. It, to him, was madness!

Shortly after he accused Paul of being mad, though, his companion, King Agrippa, said he was almost convinced that what Paul was saying was true!

What began as an inquiry into a disturbance had turned into a Gospel meeting, and when they examined Paul, they could find no error in his doctrine, and they could find no legitimate point of law on which to hold him!

Paul, by supernatural eyesight, was able to peer into the spirit and withdraw awesome truths to confound the wisdom of the wise.

CHAPTER 9:

YOUR SUPERNATURAL EYESIGHT

When we talk about taking supernatural eyesight and making it a reality in your life, we first must answer a question that is integral to understanding supernatural eyesight: What is faith?

The easy answer is that faith is the substance of things hoped for, the evidence of things not seen.

We've discussed supernatural eyesight in the past, but do we really understand it?

There's a wealth of incredible information in the New Testament that describes the state of the church today.

When the disciples doubted, Jesus called them a name that doesn't often get translated well into English Bibles.

He called them "little-faith."

He did not call them "no faith."

For instance, when He told the disciples to get into a boat and go to the other side of the sea, in the middle of the night, the boat was tossed about with a storm.

The disciples looked over the edge of the boat and saw Jesus walking on the water toward them.

The disciples got scared and said amongst themselves that what they were seeing was a ghost. The Greek word translates best into our English as "phantasm."

They were afraid it was a ghost in the worst sense of the word — they thought it was an apparition of something terrible.

Jesus, however, spoke to them from His position on the water and said, "Don't be afraid, I AM!"

Peter, apparently the bravest of the lot, still wasn't convinced, and he said, "Lord, if it's really You, command me to come meet you on the water."

When Jesus did command him, Peter walked on the water too until he got distracted and began to sink.

Jesus caught him and said, "Little-faith, why did you doubt?"

Peter had enough faith to walk on the water for a little while, but when he stood back for a second, he looked at the wind and the waves and had a sudden realization — what I'm doing is impossible.

He had faith to do a little.

He walked on the water, but when the reality of physical law came crashing down into his brain, Peter's brain could no longer suspend the natural reality that man can't walk on water, and his little faith was not enough to keep him on top of the water.

So Jesus called him "little-faith."

Most English Bibles translate "little-faith" as something like "ye of little faith."

But it means the same thing: you have *a little faith* — just not quite enough.

When we have "little-faith," we tend to get down on ourselves and begin to feel guilty.

But we've got to understand, there's a very good basis for having "little faith." The world we live in is very real to us. Gravity, in case you haven't checked lately, still works. We're still denser than water, and therefore we sink when we enter water.

Having "little faith" is only *natural.* That's why, when we believe the unbelievable, it's called super*natural* eyesight! It is GREATER than natural! It has AUTHORITY over natural!

The laws of physics are real, and from the time we were born, we were bound to obey them — and if we remain natural, until the day we die, we'll obey them.

It's only natural for terminally ill people to die.

It's only natural for dead people to stay dead.

It's only natural for people in water to sink unless they swim.

Those are all well-established facts and laws of nature — it's only natural!

When Jesus was talking to the disciples before He was delivered up to be tried, He told them they would all be offended.

Peter looked at Him and said, "No way, Lord. Everyone else may deny you, but I never will."

It's easy when you're in the presence of God to have faith.

Looking Jesus in the eye, it was easy to have faith in Him and believe in Him.

With One who walks on water, who commands the wind and the waves, who commands devils, who heals the sick and raises the dead, who speaks with such great authority, it's easy to believe anything is possible.

When Peter had his eyes on Jesus, it was easy to walk on the water — but reality came crashing in as soon as he stopped looking at Jesus.

Similarly, when Peter was looking at Jesus, it was easy to say, "No way, I'll never deny you."

But when Jesus was apprehended by a big mob armed with clubs and swords, reality came crashing in — it was only natural.

Suddenly, it wasn't so easy to believe. He still had a little faith, I'm sure, but the reality that clubs and swords could easily kill him ingrained into his brain was much more powerful than his faith.

One of the sure things in life is that you can always expect the world to continue behaving as it always has. The sun will set tonight, and it will rise tomorrow.

Water from lakes, rivers, streams and the oceans will evaporate. They'll condense into clouds, and when the water molecules in the clouds get too heavy, they'll fall to the earth as rain.

Gravity will continue to pull you toward the planet — you're not going to be suddenly flying up into space anytime soon because of a gravity failure.

When your diaphragm contracts, your lungs will pull in oxygen and convert it into nutrients the cells of your body need to survive. Those cells will send back waste, and when your diaphragm expands again, your lungs will exhale carbon dioxide.

The natural world has always worked, and we can expect it to continue working.

It is ingrained in our brains — many of the functions of life we take for granted are based upon the *faith* — there's that word — that is ingrained into our brains that the natural world will continue to operate as it always has. We DO have a little faith — we believe the world will always operate as it's supposed to.

When you wad up a piece of paper and toss it into the trash can, you're able to do that because your brain can effortlessly calculate the force of gravity, the distance between you and the can and the weight of the piece of paper relative to its mass. In a split second, your brain calculates the amount of force necessary to propel the wad of paper on the correct trajectory to make it to the trash can before gravity pulls it to earth.

In making those calculations, your brain is depending on gravity to work. It's depending on air resistance to be constant. It's depending on your muscles to obey when it commands them. It's depending on the stereoscopic vision of your eyes to accurately discern the amount of distance between you and your target.

Your brain **HAS FAITH** that none of these **NATURAL** factors has changed since the last time you threw a wad of paper into a trash can.

So when someone comes and tells you that, through Jesus, you can defy the physical laws your brain depends on for daily life, it's easy to — in your mind — say, "Yes! I believe."

But when it comes to actually putting your life, limb and reputation at risk, believing becomes a different matter.

Your brain is not quite ready to give up its hold on reality.

Do you believe you could walk on water? Many believe they could. But get them to the edge of the lake and they might have a different answer.

How then, do we allow God to increase our faith? We all have a little faith. How do we allow Him to increase it to the size of a mustard seed?

The Bible says, as we learned in chapter 7, "faith comes by hearing."

The *true reality* is that God created the universe, the world and all the laws of physics that we count on.

Gravity exists because God created it.

The sun rises because the earth rotates — and the earth rotates because God told it to.

We breathe because God created us to draw nutrients from the air around us — which He also created.

Time passes in a linear fashion because God created it to.

Mountains stay right where they are because God created them that way.

Fig trees bloom, blossom and regenerate year after year because God created them to work that way.

Humans catch diseases and die because God created our bodies to be vulnerable to them.

Humans who die stay dead because God instituted the second law of thermodynamics, which states that order descends to disorder — that which once is dead does not come back to life.

But the one who creates is also the Lord of that which He created.

Gravity pulls us toward the center of the planet because God created it to do that.

But He is Lord of gravity by virtue of having created it. Gravity must obey Him, because He is Lord.

Mountains sit where He placed them because He created them to stay there — but they also must obey Him because He is Lord.

Water sucks us in and drowns us because He created it to work that way — but when He exercises Lordship over it, the water must obey Him, not the nature He created for it.

Nature is simply another word for the normal order of the things He created. *Supernatural* is God exercising lordship over His creation and commanding it to operate outside the nature He created for it.

100-year-old people do not give birth to babies.

Water does not turn to blood.

Seas do not split wide open to allow people to pass.

Water doesn't just spring forth from a rock.

Food doesn't just accumulate on the ground every night.

An old man holding up his arms does not cause an army to win battles.

Pillars of fire and smoke don't just wander around the desert leading millions of dusty people.

Thick city walls don't just fall down flat.

Armies don't just lay down their arms to three hundred men, thinking they hear a multitude.

The sun doesn't just stand still because a man told it to.

One man can't kill a thousand with nothing but a bone.

Rocks from slings don't kill battle-hardened warriors who are nine feet tall.

People thrown into furnaces burn up.

People thrown into lion's dens get eaten.

Iron doesn't float.

Fire doesn't just come down from heaven to consume a sacrifice.

A jar of oil doesn't just keep duplicating itself.

Dead boys don't get up and walk around.

Ravens don't just feed people.

Rain doesn't stop for three years because a man told it to.

It certainly doesn't start up again because a man wanted it to.

Dipping in a dirty river doesn't cure leprosy.

Donkeys don't talk.

Touching a dead man's bones doesn't make dead people get back up.

Water does not become wine without grapes.

The blind don't just start to see because someone put His hands on them.

The deaf don't just start to hear.

Lepers don't just walk away with good skin because they were touched.

Blood doesn't just stop flowing because the person bleeding touched someone's pants.

Big storms don't just stop because someone talks to them.

People can't walk on water.

The dead don't get up from the grave after four days just because someone yells at them.

When ears are cut off, you can't just put them back on.

Shackles don't just fall off and prisons open up.

Poisonous snakes kill when they bite.

None of those things happen in the natural world.

It's just not natural.

But God created the natural — He is LORD OF IT.

The natural *MUST OBEY HIM.*

So when we're confronted with attempting to do the supernatural, our bodies and our minds resist because our bodies and minds are inextricably linked to this natural world — they are part of it, and they are prisoner to it.

Faith comes when we understand that this world is only as real as God allows it to be.

Supernatural eyesight is realizing that this natural world only works that way because a SUPERNATURAL God told it to — and when He wants it to operate differently — IT *MUST!*

Water only sucks you in and drowns you UNTIL GOD TELLS IT NOT TO.

This natural world behaves like it does because it is obeying God. But if God tells it to behave differently, it must obey Him then, too!

The real world is only real as long as it is not being acted upon by God. Our faith brings God into action on our behalf, because Jesus said if we ask something in faith, it will happen.

When we were of this world, we belonged to it. In other words, when we belonged to the world, we had to obey it. We had to obey the natural order of things. We had to sink in the water. We had to die when we got sick. We had to stay dead when we died.

We had to do those things because we were subject to the world — we were its servants.

But when we were bought by Jesus, we became servants NOT of the world — but of the living God who is Lord of the world!

We don't serve the world anymore — we serve the one the world must obey!

As His adopted sons and heirs, the world MUST ALSO OBEY US!

Here's what the Bible says:

"And returning early to the city, He hungered. And seeing one fig tree by the road, he went up to it, and found nothing on it except leaves only. And He said to it, Let there be no more fruit from you forever. And the fig tree immediately dried up. And seeing, the disciples marveled, saying, How quickly the fig tree is dried up. And answering Jesus said to them, Truly, I say to you, if you have faith and do not doubt, not only will you do the miracle of the fig tree, but even if you should say to this mountain, Be taken up and thrown into the sea — it will be so."   *Matthew 21:18-21*

Fig trees don't just dry up like that. But Jesus is the Lord of the way things act. When He speaks, everything must obey.

As His brothers who were brought into His family through His grace, He told us if we have faith and don't doubt, the natural world must obey us, too.

So I return to the beginning. We have a "little faith". *But our faith in God is hampered by our faith in this world.*

This world behaves like it does because we have not commanded it to behave otherwise.

The sick die because our faith in the world is greater than our faith in God.

We sink in the water because we believe in the water too much to understand it must obey us.

The dead stay dead because we believe in death too much to command it to let them go.

We remain "little-faith" because we believe in the power of the world.

But you can't serve two masters.

We are no longer servants of the world — it now must obey us.

When we find ourselves confronted by the impossible, if we find ourselves believing it's impossible, that's not the time to try to drum up faith inside ourselves.

Instead, it's time to realize that we don't have faith and to understand that lack of faith is indication that we have a problem — Lord, increase my faith!

No matter how hard you concentrate, you'll never be able to create faith in yourself.

You can't quote scriptures like something out of a magic book and expect it to change things.

You can't claim something you don't believe and expect it to come to pass simply by virtue of the fact that you "spoke it into existence."

Faith is the substance of things hoped for and the evidence of things not seen.

That means faith is a manifestation of the hope you have within yourself — the hope in Christ!

Faith is a FRUIT of our hope in Christ. It's not something you can work up in yourself. It's not something I can inspire by cheering you on.

Faith is the evidence of things not seen — it is the manifestation of the things we don't see! It's the evidence that Jesus is indwelling; that He's working in your life!

We don't have faith because we think we're somebody. We have faith because we understand that He is in us and His power is absolute. The natural world must obey us because it must obey Him.

Supernatural eyesight comes as evidence of that truth in our lives — not as the result of trying to get yourself to have faith. Supernatural eyesight is not the goal — it's the RESULT of hoping in Him.

You picked up this book because you wanted to know how to have supernatural eyesight — how to see things in the Spirit that are, as the Bible says, are mysteries.

Supernatural eyesight is simply understanding who God is, and understanding, as David understood when he confronted Goliath, that the natural world must obey the supernatural God.

It is knowing, as the woman with the issue of blood knew, that *this world seems real to us because our minds have faith in it* — but if our faith in God is greater, there is nothing in this world that is impossible to you.

It's having the reality in your spirit, as Moses did, that God's desire is to have a living, vibrant, intimate relationship with us, and through that relationship, to form supernatural eyesight in us that allows us to see things that no one else sees.

It's knowing, as Abraham did, that when God calls, our only correct choice is saying, Yes, Lord.

Supernatural eyesight is understanding, as Jacob did, that even when adversity — such as having his hip dislocated — strikes, holding onto Jesus is the only hope we have! It is the transition from "heel-grabber" to "power with God!"

It is understanding, as Paul did, that the former things that meant so much to you are worthless in the face of the living God who created them all. It's knowing that, no matter what you know, you are not yet perfect, and your calling beckons you to PRESS IN FURTHER.

Supernatural eyesight is understanding, as Moses did, that no matter how deep you get into God, no matter how intimate your relationship with Him, no matter how profound your understanding, there is always more — there is always another level to get to in God.

Supernatural eyesight is gained by giving up your faith in the natural world and giving up everything that holds you to this world. It is completely immersing yourself in Jesus and depending upon Him as the Source of all blessing in your life.

It is seeking Him with all your heart, all your mind, all your soul and all your spirit!

Supernatural eyesight is simple to achieve, if you follow Jesus' words:

" All things are delivered unto me of my Father: and no man knoweth the Son, but the Father; neither knoweth any man the Father, save the Son, and he to whomsoever the Son will reveal him. Come unto me, all ye that labour and are heavy laden, and I will give you rest. Take my yoke upon you, and learn of me; for I am meek and lowly in heart: and ye shall find rest unto your souls. For my yoke is easy, and my burden is light."   *Matthew 11:27-30*